Dance Histories

A Journey Across the Muslim Silk Road

First published in the UK by Beacon Books and Media Ltd

www.BeaconBooks.net

Cataloging-in-Publication record for this book is available from the British Library

ISBN 978-1-915025-80-7 Paperback
ISBN 978-1-915025-81-4 Hardback
ISBN 978-1-915025-82-1 Ebook

Cover concept by Damask Media
Cover photo by Najib Hameedi
Cover design by Raees Khan

Image credits:
The publishers would like to thank the author for providing the photographs in the book as well as the following contributors:
p.12, p.90, p.92, p.94 Kamila Erkaboyeva
p.60, p.88 Christopher Wilton-Steer
p.72 Diana Takutdinova
p.102 El Funoun
p.108 Hawiyya Dance Company
p.116 & p.122 Najib Hameedi
p. 142, p.146 Omar Al-Badry
p. 152 Kinding Sindaw

Dance Histories

A Journey Across the Muslim Silk Road

Nadia Khan

Dear Frank

Thank you for your continued support & encouragement

Nadia

BEACON BOOKS

Contents

Introduction – A Journey of Self Discovery

Dance is a powerful connection to our past, and certainly to mine. It has been the vehicle through which I have learnt more about myself and my family, and consequently my history and heritage.

From a young age, I have always loved to dance and been curious about the past. History was one of my favourite subjects, and I loved reading English classical novels, watching period dramas and old films. Dance and history, I have discovered, go hand in hand as dance also traces the stories of the past. At university I read History for both my Bachelor's and Master's degrees. My specialism is in the Indian partition of 1947. I also write and blog about shared cultures and histories of the Muslim world, and beyond, through my project

'Golden Threads', set up in 2020; the year in which the Covid pandemic shook the world.

During my studies and working life, I continued to pursue my love of dance in my 'down time'. I spent holidays and weekends choreographing dances for Muslim cultural events, weddings and henna parties, and also just for fun. This hobby has been one of the constants in my life, and has exposed me to different world music and cultures which I have a deep connection with to this day. It's almost impossible for me to hear music from the Muslim world or anything with a good beat, and not think about choreography in my head.

My life journey thus far, reading and interests have led me to write this book. It is a natural progression of my creative spirit and love of dance, combined with my desire to understand the world and learn more about previous societies and people. As a result of researching this book, I was able to explore my faith and culture in much more detail as well as my family's story, and that has been an invaluable experience. As the great African-American poet and writer Maya Angelou says, "You can't really know where you are going until you know where you have been."

Dance plays a huge role in my own Indo-Pakistani cultural heritage and also my Muslim heritage. This might seem strange to some as dance can be a controversial and loaded topic in the Muslim community. However, through the pages of this book, I will explore the rich culture of dance that has existed for centuries. I will also explore how Muslim dance has travelled along the Silk Road and has led to many shared features across Muslim cultures. These connections are intrinsic to history, and more specifically to the history of Muslim trade and migration. I will also reflect on how this past is part of my story. For example, according to current race classifications, I am ethnically 'Pakistani', but like many in Pakistan, have long-standing connections to India, as Partition only took place in 1947. My story is more than man-made borders. The history and heritage of Muslims in India stretches back over a thousand years as Muslims first arrived on Indian shores in the eighth century, led by Arab leader Muhammad bin Qasim, who established the Islamic province of Sindh. Since then, there have been many other Muslim rulers from Afghanistan, Central Asia, Persia and from Turkic cultures that have left a legacy in South Asia.

Music and dance feature prominently in the Indian subcontinent. They are a core part of the culture, although their meanings and use have inevitably evolved over time. For those living in the diaspora, music and dance are important ways of staying connected to one's heritage. This is exactly how my family kept connected to their homeland after migrating to the UK, along with language, clothes and food.

In 1962, my mum (Khalida Khan), her two siblings, parents and extended family arrived in London from Pakistan, driving in a Bedford van through Afghanistan, Iran, Turkey and Europe. In the 1960s, you could do this relatively safely and easily. My mum tells me of amazing adventures, like something out of an Agatha Christie novel, minus the drama and intrigue. I still imagine beautiful landscapes, Middle Eastern sounding music, bazaars and warm colours when I hear the story. The people they met along the way were welcoming and generous, a nod to the famous hospitality Muslims are renowned for. They joined my paternal great-grandfather who was already in London. He arrived in the 1950s and was living in a run-down area of Old Street, East London, which ironically now is a trendsetter's paradise with unaffordable house prices. It's not a place they would ever be able to live if they arrived now.

My mum suffered a lot of racist and Islamophobic abuse in 1960s London which affected her deeply. These experiences encouraged her to hold on to her heritage more tightly and ignited a passion to fight inequality. She thus became a race advisor, community activist and founder of An-Nisa Society, in 1985. This is a well-known and established charity led by Muslim women, for the past forty years it has been working to support Muslim families and address social exclusion and Islamophobia. They broke patriarchal boundaries and contributed to shaping British Islam as we know it. My mum also set up a supplementary Muslim school around the same time, which is still in operation after almost forty years. My mum's vision was to work for all Muslim communities, regardless of race or cultural background. She saw Islam as a unifying factor, trying to adhere to the Islamic principle that we are all equal in the eyes of God, which is the ethos underpinning An-Nisa Society.

I grew up in this multicultural Islam. My uncle, Fuad Nahdi, was the founder and editor of the renowned Muslim magazine, Q News. My mother also wrote articles for the magazine and my whole family were heavily involved in it. We

• Opposite page, Farida Maqbul (Nani) and Manzoor Hussain Khan (Papa), my grandparents with the famous pigeons in Trafalgar Square in the 1960s.

• This page, Nani in London and Nani with her children, including my mother.

had Muslim friends and family of different cultural backgrounds from all corners of the globe. This was the norm for me, and still is. I was very much aware that there was a wondrous variety of cultures and people in the world, and from the perspective of my Islamic faith, this was a deliberate and beautiful act of God. The Qur'an says, "People, We created you all from a single man and a single woman, and made you into peoples and tribes so that you should recognize one another."[1]

As a result of this multi-culturalism, my upbringing was vibrant and colourful. Dance was a prominent feature at weddings and celebrations. As a child, I was mesmerised by the dance aesthetics of the Muslim world, the elegant and graceful moves, the sound of the music and the vibrant dress. The dances were mainly performed in a female-only context within our circles, and the women were so happy and confident, connected to the music and to themselves. The dance bonded women of all ages; we would dance with our grandmothers, mums and aunts in sheer happiness. It was then that I fell in love with dance and this passion has stayed with me to this day.

Although the dance styles I witnessed from around the world varied from my own cultural background, there were also some similarities in movement, style and dress. It was as if a common thread of Islamic culture ran through the heart of these dance forms. I am thrilled that I now have the chance to explore this connection on a deeper level.

1-The Evolution of Dance

The first historical proof of dance comes from nine-thousand-year-old paintings found in primitive caves in India. There are also accounts of structured dancing used by ancient Egyptian priests for storytelling purposes in both religious ceremonies and for entertainment.

Throughout time people developed dance for a variety of reasons: to liven up mundane tasks, collective activity, celebration, worship and of course storytelling. Dance was a part of how they lived; not quite like a Bollywood movie, but part of their daily existence. The result has been the effortlessly beautiful creations which we value to this day, and which act as a mouthpiece of a society and culture.

Another beautiful quality of dance is that it can transcend barriers and differences, and provide a way to connect with our community, environment and spiritual essence. Sonia Hinz in her PhD thesis, *Dance, Mysticism, and*

Sensuality Perspectives from Tajikistan says, "Dance and music together provide an emotional, psychological, or spiritual release from everyday problems."[2]

John Martin, a twentieth-century dance critic, described dance as a physical expression of inner emotion. He said, "At the root of all these varied manifestations of dancing... lies the common impulse to resort to movement to externalise states which we cannot externalise by rational means. This is basic dance."[3] In essence, dance is born from our inner selves, or our spirituality, if you like.

From the nineteenth and twentieth centuries, dance along the Silk Road regions became an acclaimed art form for elite dancers and a nationalistic construction, with a focus on choreographed performance to entertain. Although these performances are beautiful and serve as a means to bring people together for art and nation building, they are not the origins of these dances. This is found in grassroots communities, and is part and parcel of collective identity. The beauty is that everyone can participate, from the very young to the very old. Historically, dance has not always been reserved for performance but has been used by communities for a variety of purposes; this is known as 'folk dance'. For the context of this book, I will use the term folk dance to refer to traditional dances of rural and tribal communities.

As dance is a form of human expression, it is inspired by people and their environment. This is why dance has a lot of regional variations but also shares similarities in certain shared cultures or what were once empires. One can see these similarities across Muslim lands stemming from Arabia, then spreading out through Persia, Central Asia, South Asia and Europe. I will chart this in detail on our journey across the Silk Road.

The existence of shared dance forms in the Muslim world was explored and confirmed by the late scholar, Lois Ibsen al-Faruqi. She conducted extensive research on Muslim dance and is the most authoritative voice on this little-explored subject. She states, "Dance did not play the important aesthetic role in Islamic civilization that it played in some other civilizations... The Muslims were never able to quite resolve the uncertainty which they, as a people, felt over the legitimacy of dance."[4]

Despite this hesitation over dance in the public arena, the Muslim world does dance, and has produced some beautiful dance forms, and there are similarities between some of them based on a shared Islamic core and culture. The influence of music, and subsequently dance, from the Muslim world has impacted even non-Muslim dance forms such as flamenco, which was born out of Muslim rule in Spain which lasted for almost eight hundred years. This is a testament to the existence of a Muslim dance form and its artistry.

The dances that are most common, according to Lois Ibsen al-Faruqi, are combat dances to prepare for battle; solo improvisational dances; chain or line dances and religious dances of the Muslim brotherhoods. Lois Ibsen al-Faruqi asserts that these are the four common categories of dance that appear consistently across the Muslim world. "Certain characteristics of content and structure apply generally to the dances of the Muslim peoples from widely dispersed geographic areas. These are its abstract quality; its improvisatory nature; its emphasis on small, intricate movements; its serial structure, and its unfolding of a series of mini-climaxes. These common features suggest that there is a basic artistic unity in the art of dance among Muslims which is comparable to that acknowledged by numerous Muslim and non-Muslim scholars to be discernible in the visual arts of Islamic culture."[5]

Lois Ibsen al-Faruqi likens the essence of Muslim dance culture to other Islamic arts such as architecture and literature, which are commonly accepted as being influenced by Islamic philosophy and teachings. She states, "Whether we investigate the poetry, the visual arts, or the music, we find the division of an artistic product in Islamic culture pulling the spectator or listener through a labyrinth of intricate details, each with its planned denouement."[6]

Dance in the Islamic world has a spiritual core according to Lois Ibsen al-Faruqi's work, and some forms are influenced by aspects of Islamic art and geometry. Muslim dance has developed different uses over time, as it has evolved from its origins in small village style communities. After the industrial revolutions, the world changed dramatically and people began to move out in large numbers from rural communities to find work in newly-built cities. Dance in Muslim communities subsequently evolved from a close-knit community activity based on everyday tasks and religious rituals, to being more structured. However, the movements in modern dance still have an imprint of the past, mainly because it became a means of staying connected to home and traditions. When people moved even further afield and emigrated, they held onto the past even more strongly.

Folk dance also retained its place in modern society,[7] but started to be used more commonly, even in Muslim countries, as a nation-building tool. Dance has consequently become more valued and accepted in Muslim society. However, this grey area about the moral acceptability of dance still exists in the Muslim community, and especially in traditional and rural societies. Dance continues to be seen as a non-respectable profession, especially for women.

In the 'Christian-Western' world, there were also differing religious positions around the permissibility of dance. There were ritual dances used for religious worship by some faith leaders, whereas others frowned upon it. Christianity, like Islam, has traditionally been critical of any public displays that might be considered sexually provocative. But, unlike Islam, Christianity also has to navigate what some see as its critical or ambivalent attitude towards sensual pleasures per se (especially sexual pleasure), which naturally has a bearing on how dance is perceived. This strict attitude has varied somewhat in both Christian and Muslim lands, depending on the rulers' convictions to stamp out 'frivolous' dance practices.

In the West, there was a growing social dance tradition, court dances and formal structured dances, such as ballet, which became recognised as art forms. With colonialism, post-colonialism and the growth of nationalism, dance and its practice evolved further. Some Muslim countries such as Central Asia, Iran and Turkey started to see a growth in classical Western dance forms such as ballet, as there was a desire to imitate the more 'advanced' Western world.

In both the Christian and Muslim empires, even when dance started to become popular in the courtly settings and patronised by monarchs, there was still a time when both societies saw dance as a profession for socially and morally inferior persons. It is interesting to note that this disapproving attitude towards dance, throughout history, was not just limited to the Islamic context. Islamic teachings do not actually prohibit dance or sensual movements, but some are disapproving of 'inappropriate' mixed-sex dancing and performance by women in the public arena. But this is not a straightforward permissible or non-permissible (halal or haram) view on dance, and has its nuances.

Dr. Laurel Victoria Gray, Artistic Director of the Silk Road Dance Company, echoes the view that Islam does not prohibit sensual movement, but it needs to be within an appropriate context. When it is appropriate, it is generally not viewed negatively. She sheds light on why the Orientalist fantasy was created when observing Muslim women dance. She says, "We as a culture (in the West) need to accept sexuality as elegant, as a positive force; that is provocative without being pornographic, erotic without being vulgar, sensuous without being debased."[8] Therefore, Muslim women expressing themselves in a sensual way within a female-only context, carries no negative connotations in Islam. However, it has been taken from its context and used to depict Muslim societies and women in a barbaric, oversexed and uncivilised way.

• Uyghur dancer

2- What's the Controversy over Muslim Dance?

There is a lack of academic and other written work on traditional Muslim dance cultures and history. However, I am committed to tell the story of dance across Muslim society and cultures, and unravel a rich spiritual and artistic heritage that is either ignored, written out of history due to anti-Muslim sentiment or perverted by Orientalist[9] illusions.

Dance in the Muslim world has commonly been seen as forbidden by Muslim orthodoxy, or the other end of the spectrum - an Orientalist image of semi-naked women performing sexualised belly dance movements in front of an audience of men. There is no happy or realistic medium. This picture is a travesty to the legacy of dance culture across the Muslim world and beyond. I want to rescue dance from this narrative that completely destroys the tasteful, artistic, elegant, spiritual and social ritual of dance in the Muslim world.

My research has led me to the conclusion that many traditional dances across the Muslim world have a direct connection to the Divine. I'm referring to the combination of movements which are inspired by God and His creation, and lyrics and accompanying music which are in praise of the Creator. Traditional dance, like other aspects of Muslim art and culture, has been influenced by Islamic philosophy but due to a lack of academic research or discussion on this topic, the connection to dance is neglected. It is easier to recognise the very visual impact of Islamic thought on Muslim architecture, literature, poetry, music, fashion and other arts.

The Prophet Muhammad said, "God is beautiful and He loves beauty." This concept of 'beauty' is reflected across Islamic civilisation and the Muslim effort to create a reflection of paradise on earth. As the author and scholar Recip Dogan observes, "In Islamic thought, everything is surrounded by infinite beauty. The source of beauty is faith and with perspective Muslims conceive of everything as beautiful."[10] Therefore the beauty has meaning and purpose, and is a reflection of the 'Oneness' of God. It is not 'art for art's sake'.[11]

The beauty of traditional Muslim dance goes deeper than aesthetics alone, and in societies where God and faith are integral, the dance movements created were influenced by this connection to a higher purpose, and in some cases mirrored other Muslim art forms such as symmetry and geometry. Sonia Hinz writes about this connection in her PhD thesis *Dance, Mysticism, and Sensuality Perspectives from Tajikistan*, "This aesthetic (lateral symmetry in dance) rooted in rhythm, the circle (in this case, referring to turning, spinning, circular and curvilinear motion - all derived from the circle), repetition, and symmetry is based on the geometrical foundation of Islamic calligraphy, which often acts as a model for other Islamic arts (Gocer 1999). Interestingly, Gocer hypothesizes that this aesthetic is spiritually and morally based (1999). His argument links Islamic and Platonic aesthetics, and he asserts this aesthetic basis is grounded in the belief of God's Perfection, Beauty, and Harmony, which should be reflected in art; thus, art that adheres to this aesthetic contributes to moral and spiritual well being."[12]

In this line of belief, God's beauty is seen to be present in sound and music. Many Sufis believe that nature is a form of music and they use these natural sounds in their quest to connect with the Divine. Sufism is the mystical form of Islam and focuses on an inward connection with God. Sufi leader, Sefik Can, in his book *Fundamentals of Rumi's Thought*, quotes the poet Rumi, "We have taken these beautiful sounds and melodies from the whirling of the heavens. These pleasant sounds that people produce with musical instruments or their voices are taken from the rotation of the heavens. We heard those melodies while we were in Heaven... It is for this reason that music and whirling is nourishment for lovers of God."[13]

There is an ongoing debate within the fold of Islam about the permissibility of music. However, if one believes that nature contains music and is part of God's creation, music is thus allowed and can in fact be spiritual. Sefik Can asserts that music is not disallowed in Islam, and provides evidence from hadiths[14] where the Prophet Muhammad himself witnessed music and dance and did not eschew it. He says, "'Islam does not prohibit music. In fact, in the Glorious Qur'an the beautiful voice is praised while the ugly voice is renounced. It is narrated that the Prophet permitted some of the dances that he watched. It is also known that when our Prophet and his Companion Abu Bakr left Makka and honoured Medina, some of the women of Medina greeted them, singing the poem Tala al-badru alayna ("A full moon has risen over us") and playing tambourines.'"[15]

Thus, worshipping God and reflecting on His creation takes many forms and is not only a ritualistic act reserved for the prayer mat or mosque. It includes observing nature, working the land, celebrating happy occasions and going to battle. The dance movements that flow from these day-to-day events take God as inspiration. In societies where religion plays a central role, it makes sense that religious ideals would play a part in shaping dance of all genres, and not just Sufi practices.

When looking at Muslim dance in this context of everyday activity, nature and beauty, the spiritual element, which holds God at the centre, is clear. As Sonia Hinz states, dance is impacted by Islamic concepts because of "the deep permeation of the Islamic ideology into every aspect of Muslim life."[16] This realisation has allowed me to re-evaluate orthodox perceptions of dance in Islamic communities. I want to urge others to do the same, or at the very least, consider an alternative view of how dance was practised and developed.

There are clearly divided opinions about dancing and music in Muslim communities but this is not necessarily an issue or unexpected. It only becomes problematic when the extreme conservative Muslim and Orientalist views, which have for many years dominated this area of study, mask the rich history of dance in the Muslim world and its spiritual connection.

It is also a great a shame that negative views of dance in the Muslim world has led to the prohibition of some of the oldest and most beautiful traditional dance styles in countries such as Iran and Afghanistan. This has threatened the preservation of these dances. It is, therefore, imperative to record our own history and heritage, including our lost dance stories.

THE ROLE OF WOMEN

Muslim women love to dance, at least from my experience of cultural events, henna parties and weddings. However, there is a grey cloud hovering over this whole subject, not only from the Orientalist sexualisation of the Muslim woman, but also patriarchal views towards women and their bodies.

I have witnessed a rich dance culture in the Muslim world during my travels. However, as I mentioned earlier, the history and existence of some of the dances is hard to find in the mainstream.

In a Muslim religious context, dance is not strictly prohibited. The main contention in orthodox Muslim circles is sensual dance by females in public, or mixed-sex dancing. In Islam, women dancing amongst other women is completely acceptable. Mixed-sex dance forms consequently come into direct conflict with orthodox views of dance in Islam. However, as I have already mentioned, there are a variety of views in the Muslim world about this subject and when it comes to folk dancing, views about women, dance and mixing can be more relaxed. This is especially true if the dance is within a family context.

Dr. Laurel Victoria Gray, Artistic Director of the Silk Road Dance Company, who has contributed heavily to the preservation of dance histories of the Silk Road, has added a fifth theme of dance seen in the Muslim world in addition to Lois Ibsen al-Faruqi's four categories. This is known the 'couple dance'; although she states it's more rare, it consists of both same and opposite sex partners and can be seen predominantly in Turkey. Therefore, we do see mixed-sex dancing in some cultures and areas.

Dance performances by women, for the entertainment of men, was practised in courtly and other private settings throughout history. However, it was never a socially acceptable practice, and was often done behind closed doors. The dancing women were often of low social class and looked down upon. These practices are depicted in poetry, literature and more recently, films. There are some Bollywood movies, such as *Pakeezah* (1972) and *Umrao Jann* (1982), that have told stories about these dancing women or courtesans, who performed for the pleasure of princes across India. Some of these women were taught poetry, literature and became quite learned, and they were able to impress their male audience with their intellectual talents as well as their sensuousness. However, despite this, their position was not elevated.

The erotic style of dance performed by women, for men in seedy establishments definitely increased the negative view of dance in respectable society. As it was frowned upon for women to dance in front of men, public dance performances were dominated by men or young boys. This can be seen commonly in the Middle Eastern dance styles of dabke, sword dances and the spiritual dances of the whirling dervishes. However, in recent years, women can also be seen performing these traditional dances alongside men.

There are accounts in history of Muslim women taking part in spiritual dances such as the sema. Early female Sufis such as Rabi'ah al-Adawiyya from the eighth century, female disciples of Rumi in the thirteenth century and Mughal princesses wrote Sufi poetry. There is evidence that some of these women performed the Sufi sema as well, so it is quite possible that women participating in dance, especially spiritual dance, is not a new phenomenon. Camille Helminski writes, "'Women have also always performed the sema, the mystical whirling ceremony of the Mevlevi Way. In the early days of the Mevlevi order, women and men were known to pray, share sohbet (spiritual conversation), and whirl within each other's company, though more often as the centuries unfolded, women held their own semas and men also whirled in dhikr separately from women. However, in the time of Mevlana, spontaneous semas would occur including both women and men."[17] Dance amongst women is actually promoted within the framework of the Muslim religion. Dr Gray says,

"In traditional Silk Road cultures, women dance for each other, at parties, and at celebrations; I find Western women are hungry for this feminine expression. In one workshop I teach, 'The Enlightenment of the Body,' women find the space that allows them to embrace and accept their femininity; it becomes a road of exploration, one of celebration, where there is no competition, judgement or shame. This dance actually transforms women."[18]

Dance for Muslim women within an all-female environment, has long been a way to express themselves, promote feminine health and boost self-esteem. It is seen as a positive practice and has been passed on from generation to generation. Belly dance, for example, has a long history in the Middle East, and contains movements of the hips, upper body, graceful arm movements and often performed in ordinary or traditional clothes. Sensual movements are present, but are completely acceptable within a Muslim context, just not in public.

Belly dancing as a heavily sexualised, boundary-pushing dance as we see it in its current form, is a much more modern phenomenon. The style we see now is said to have been popular in Egyptian nightclubs in the early twentieth century, initially focused on the entertainment of men. I often wonder how much this Orientalist fantasy of scantily clad, exotic Muslim women, dancing in the harems for the 'lustful Muslim men', fed into the actual creation of this fantasy in real life by the very cultures that it exploited? At the time belly dancing in nightclubs was becoming popular, colonial control and influence was still embedded in these eastern lands. It would be plausible that the entertainment and night life that was created, was largely to cater to the Western audiences. Why not provide the orientalists their fantasy and make money from it?

On the other hand, there was also a growing desire for eastern people to copy Western culture once the Muslim world was in decline, because they saw it as modern and progressive. Some Muslim communities themselves took steps to move away from traditional practices, such as women-only dancing, and were keen to experiment with Western dance styles.

Such is the popularity of belly dance now that it is seen as one of the main cultural embodiments of Muslim, Arab, Turkish and Iranian culture. Bollywood has also embraced belly dance, and one of their most famous and popular dancers is Noor Fatehi who is of Moroccan heritage. The Columbian singer Shakira, who has Lebanese heritage, is arguably more famous for her 'my hips don't lie' belly dances than her songs. Due to the immense popularity of belly dance, it has dominated the Muslim cultural dance conversation and sadly, little is known about the traditional elegant dance forms and other beautiful dance practices across the Middle East and surrounding regions.

RECLAIMING MUSLIM IDENTITY AND DANCE

Traditional Muslim dance has significant links to faith and spirituality. Now that Muslims are living all across the world, many as minorities, in some ways they hold on stronger to their culture and faith in fear of losing it. However, with each generation, the meaning and understanding behind certain cultural or religious practices inevitably fade. This is concerning for the survival of Muslim dance traditions.

Muslim civilisation and structures were largely destroyed during colonialism and its aftermath. This has impacted our connections to history, faith and culture, especially in the diaspora. On top of that, there is the real struggle of Islamophobia and increased surveillance of Muslims, which has been documented widely across mainstream reports and data. This puts pressure on Muslim communities to practise their faith and culture without threat or prejudice.

However, at the same time it does seem that the reconnection and confidence in a Muslim identity is beginning to emerge, despite the prevailing Islamophobia around the world or perhaps as a result of it. The Muslim community is increasingly going back to its traditions and celebrating their cultural and religious identity on its own terms. This can be seen on social media where content and stories from Muslim influencers are thriving, travelling to Muslim countries such as Pakistan is becoming more popular and businesses selling a Muslim cultural experience, food and traditional arts and crafts seems to be growing. In addition, in the British mainstream there are more and more Muslim professionals, artists and performers asserting their 'Muslimness', from politicians and MPs, to actors like Riz Ahmed and comedians like Guz Khan and Big Zuu. These prominent individuals are seemingly unafraid to speak about their faith despite an atmosphere of anti-Muslim hatred and ignorance.

I see much more social media content now of Muslims dancing and promoting their cultures. Non-Muslims are also copying these dances because they are seen as trendy or fun. Although the orthodox Muslim view on music and dance still exists, it seems it no longer dominates the narrative like it did when I was growing up. There are now more Muslims on mainstream platforms, including dancers, who are confidently expressing their connection to Islam rather than trying to keep a low profile or rejecting their faith.

Social media is definitely playing a huge role in communities sharing their dance content and stories, even in remote areas of the world. I personally noticed a turning point after the launch of Pharrell Williams' music video *Happy* in 2013. Soon after its release, people around the world were using the song to create their own videos, singing and dancing along to this feel-good tune. Muslim communities were no exception. The world was able to see Muslims dancing and being joyful; a sight that many were not used to. Residents in countries such as Jordan, Senegal, Egypt, Lebanon and Sudan shared videos. Sadly, it did not go down very well in Iran, where participants were arrested, reinforcing the stereotype.

There was a British Muslim version of the 'Happy' song which went viral. Of course, there were some expected rumblings in the Muslim community, but the biggest frenzy was created by mainstream British media. Journalists were surprised at the images of singing, dancing Muslims of all ages and sexes. It was the complete opposite of the usual coverage of the Muslim community on the typical subjects of 'refugees', 'hijabs', or 'terrorism'. This dancing wasn't traditional Muslim dance per se, but it was a fusion of different cultures, and expressions of joy and faith. I think this inspired many Muslim creatives, including myself, and provided hope for a new dawn where we could be our authentic selves.

All these developments have happened in recent years. We now have the Quick Style dance group from Norway creating viral content on TikTok and social channels. The dancers are led by Pakistani-Norwegian twin brothers, Suleman and Bilal Malik, alongside their childhood friend, Nasir Sirikhan, who is Thai-Norwegian. The Quick Style choreograph dances include Muslim dance

• The Quick Style Dance Group

forms from around the world, as well as Bollywood and urban hip-hop. Many are clearly fusion dances that are mixing Muslim traditional dance with other world and modern flavours. The Quick Style founders are positively Muslim, and do not shy away from expressing their faith. They have done an amazing job of putting dance on the map from a Muslim cultural perspective. Although they may or may not be thinking about the spiritual connection of their work, the fact is that the story behind many of the traditional dances they practise is linked to a wider narrative, and they are adding their own connection to the faith in their unique way.

It is clear that an alternative voice to negative Muslim stereotypes is emerging; one that is reawakening the beauty of Muslim art and culture, including dance, within a framework of faith. Younger generations, who are proudly Muslim, are entering the mainstream using their Muslim cultural music and heritage as a backdrop, and experimenting with other forms of dance and music as well. For example, Alaa Wardi is a singer of Iranian background, who remixes Arabic and North African music with popular Western tunes. I went to see the Quick Style in concert and concepts such as the 'Oneness of God' and Islamic references, were used throughout their performance. A great deal of this reawakening has been driven by the younger generation, many living in Muslim countries and the diaspora, who are comfortable and proud of their Muslim heritage, using modern tools to express themselves and tell their own stories.

This change has inspired me to revive my love of dance. It feels like the right time to do this. I am excited to explore the stories that are overlooked or buried under negative media stereotypes, as well as orthodoxy within Muslim communities that destroys balance and different interpretations. Muslim dance culture is part of world heritage and should not be wiped out of history. Muslim dance also provides a vital insight into our lost stories and connections.

I will explore the different traditional dance cultures across the Muslim world, and see how they developed and influenced each other. For the purpose of this book, I will focus on the dance cultures of the Silk Road including Andalusia, the Arab world, Central Asia, Persia and South Asia. These are my areas of expertise, as well as the main areas where large Islamic empires existed and interacted with each other in some way, which consequently led to a sharing of music and dance styles. I will journey from East to West and explore the variety of dances, the history behind them and hear personal stories of those practising the dances today.

There are even more stories of dance to tell across many other parts of the Muslim world, and one day I hope to also explore these in more detail.

3- A Shared Islamic Culture

I wanted to begin by delving into the roots of Islamic culture and its universality. This will help the reader to understand my theory that Muslim cultural dance has a shared spiritual connection along the Silk Road. Islamic empires spread rapidly along the Silk Road trade route following the death of Prophet Muhammad in the seventh century. With this, an 'Islamic culture' developed and spread.

Why do we say Islamic culture as opposed to culture of specific Muslim countries or ethnicities? This is a question that I've always been intrigued by. Growing up, my family were very much influenced by our North Indian Muslim culture, and there are certain cultural practices which are commonplace amongst people from this area. Although much from this is inspired by Islam, it has other influences too. Islamic culture, on the other hand, stems from the spiritual connection, and principles that emanate from philosophy and teachings from the Qur'an and the Prophet Muhammad. The culture that has developed from Islamic values has a tangible as well spiritual form; it is all-inclusive and can be seen in practices such as religious festivals, fasting in Ramadan, ritual observances and external forms such as art, architecture and, in my understanding, dance.

Colonisation and its aftermath spearheaded the nationalist movement. This saw large empires of multicultural people break down into nation states. As a result, populations moved away from thinking in terms of regional and faith connections, to thinking in nationalist terms. Patriotism became the new trend, creating divisions which are still with us to this day.

Nationalist thinking has become ingrained even in the Muslim world. However, when I've travelled across different Muslim countries, there are many similarities in culture which come from Islam. For example, Muslims tend to remove their shoes before going into people's houses; hospitality to travellers is the norm because it is a teaching from the Qur'an and emphasised by the Prophet; avoiding figurative art is a common trend in Islam and Muslims do not use figures of people in mosques, so instead you will find beautiful patterns inspired by nature or geometric art.

These are just a few of the similarities in cultures across Muslim lands where religion has historically been front and centre. An Islamic culture still exists, but sometimes that obvious link to the faith has been forgotten.

GOLDEN THREAD OF ISLAMIC CULTURE

Islam is seen as a way of life, rather than just a religion. The principles and teachings in the Qur'an shape a believer's behaviour, character and moral principles but also impacts their lifestyle.

Within a few hundred years following the death of Prophet Muhammad in 632 CE, Muslim empires were formed in different regions across the world, spanning vast land masses, reaching Spain in the West and India in the east. Islam spread as far as northern Europe and the Far East. The iconic 1976 film *The Message* directed by Moustapha Akkad, tells the story of the life of the Prophet Muhammad. There is a striking scene at the end of the film which shows footage of Muslims praying all over the world in the twentieth century; a very visual depiction of how far and wide Islam has spread.

It is fascinating to explore how a religion, which originated in Arabia in the seventh century, spread to the most remote parts of the world, and not only had a huge impact on Western civilisation, but contributed to shaping it.

One of the secrets of the success of the Muslim empires was trade combined with the love of learning from others. Goods being bought and sold has long been the way of the world, and Arabs had traditionally been skilled traders, including the Prophet Muhammad. With the advent of Islam, Arab Muslims continued to trade with other lands. Many scholars suggest that this is one of the primary ways that Islamic civilisation spread across the world rather than the orientalist narrative of Islam being spread by the sword. Travelling to new lands and meeting different people, allowed Muslims to learn from others and opened up a channel for their religion and culture to reach new societies.

Muslims traded along the Silk Road, the ancient trade route, connecting Asia, Persia, Arabia, East Africa and the Mediterranean. China is trying to revive this route with their 'Belt and Road' initiative. The origins of the Silk Road can be traced back to 130 BCE. The Silk Road was not only a channel for the exchange of goods, but the sharing of religions, ideas and cultural practices. When Islam was established, Professor A. Reza Hoshmand states that, "Most Silk Road traders coming from Western Eurasia were Muslim, and as one would expect, they brought their beliefs and rich cultures to millions of people along the route."[19]

The spread of Islam happened at a time in history where political expansion and defence of territory was the norm. The dominant narrative is that Islam spread by the sword. However, mainstream scholarship in recent years has begun to challenge this view with new available historical evidence. Amongst other more plausible reasons scholars mention, one is that it could have spread by a charismatic and attractive culture, which in the early days in particular, treated minorities well. Peter Frankopan in his notable work *The Silk Road* says about Muslim empires, "The picture of enlightenment and cultural sophistication was also reflected in the way that minority religions and cultures were treated."[20]

Where early Arab Muslims established their rule, it has been argued they were not often met with hostile opposition from locals, who welcomed a change from their existing oppressive rulers. Islamic rule, where practised in line with the Prophet Muhammad's teachings, brought a system of justice and spirituality, which often resulted in a fresh change from oppressive systems and exploitation. Peter Frankopan reaffirms this point. He says, "In fact, it appears that the Arab conquests were neither as brutal nor as shocking as the commentators make out. Across Syria and Palestine, for example, there is little evidence of violent conquest in the archaeological record. Damascus, for instance, the most important city in northern Syria, surrendered quickly after terms were agreed between the local bishop and the attacking Arab commander."[21]

Contrary to the Orientalist rhetoric, the early Muslim empires did not force conversions in their newly acquired lands either, according to Peter Frankopan. "Cohabitation of the faiths was an important hallmark of early Islamic expansion–and an important part of its success."[22] The Ottoman Empire, for example, was well known for providing protection to persecuted Jews. For the seven centuries that the Muslims ruled Jerusalem uninterruptedly, beginning with the reconquest by Salah ad-Din in 1187 CE, the three Abrahamic faiths existed side by side. Forcing people to change their religion was not part of their Arab tradition and as minority rulers, they would not have succeeded for very long if they forced inhabitants to convert against their will. They also set to benefit from charging non-Muslims a tax for protection and exemption from military service or 'jizya', and widespread conversion would have lost them this extra income.

Large-scale conversion to Islam took place several hundred years after its birth and for a variety of reasons. Some could have genuinely been attracted to the Islamic message; Muslims often married into the local population which helped the spread of the religion; many people chose Islam to align with the more dominant and advanced cultural ways of the ruling empire or perhaps wanted to avoid paying the jizya tax. It could also have been that the Muslim approach of adopting indigenous traditions and embedding them within the framework of Islam, may have naturally appealed to their new subjects and made Islam seem less foreign. Sufism, the mystical arm of Islam, also had a big part to play in widespread conversion to Islam. "Part of the spread of these shifting, adaptive spiritual views was carried out by a new type of Muslim holy men acting as a form of missionary; these mystics, known as sufis... They seem to have played a crucial role in winning converts,"[23] states Frankopan.

Muslims travelled for trade and often settled in new lands; they were constantly encountering new people. This broadened their horizons and allowed them to learn from different cultures. Arabs were familiar with interacting with new people and took teachings from their own religion, as well as the knowledge they had gained in other lands, and combined these to spread knowledge and advancements across the world. The result was the creation of vibrant cultures and thriving societies, the legacy of which is still strong today.

Muslims had a compelling thirst for knowledge and learning, which was encouraged by the Qur'an as well as the Prophet Muhammed. Professor Cherif Bassiouni states, "The Arabs clearly followed the Hadith (sayings) of the Prophet urging them to pursue knowledge from birth to death, even if that search was to be in China."[24]

In the Qur'an, God says, "O humanity! Indeed, We created you from a male and female, and made you into peoples and tribes so that you may 'get to' know one another."[25] These words seemed to drive the early zealous Muslims to learn from others, and to record not only their own history and ideas, but those of other peoples. This is why at the height of the Islamic Golden Age, Muslims were seen as a conduit of knowledge and culture across the world. They were not a sedentary people. It is through the Muslims that the world learnt how to make paper, which the former first picked up from interaction with the Chinese. Muslims also introduced algebra to the world, which they formulated after learning from the works of the Greeks and ancient Indians. Muslims preserved and brought Greek philosophical learning to the world. They translated the classical works, developed them, whilst also adding their own knowledge and insights. There have been many great Muslim philosophers in their own right, such as Ibn Khaldun (d.1406), Ibn Sina (Avicenna, d.1037) and Ibn Rushd (Averroes, d.1198), who have also produced their own masterpieces. Professor Akbar S. Ahmed states, "The Arab world returned the gift of Greek learning to Europe, augmented by their own considerable achievements, which helped to trigger the European renaissance."[26] If it was not for the Muslim role in transmitting and augmenting these philosophies, it is likely that much of this history would have been lost and Europe would have remained in the Dark Ages according to many historians.

Islam may have started out in Arabia, but under the Abbasid rulers who came into power from 750 to 1258 and were based in Baghdad, it spread even further afield. The Abbasids were advocates of multiculturalism and a type of 'Pan-Islamism'[27] that covered all new lands and people. Cherif Bassiouni says, "The Abbasid rulers, unlike the Umayyads who remained Arab in their tastes and customs, conceived an Islamic polity based on religious affiliation rather than nationality or race."[28]

The expansion of Islam into Spain began with offshoots of the Umayyad Empire from 711-1031, and developed into its very own Andalusian culture based on Islam and inspired by Jewish and indigenous societies as well. Under the Abbasids, Muslim rule also spread throughout Persia, Southeast Asia and Africa. Therefore, as well as an Arab-focused culture, other forms of cultural expressions developed, but all had a common thread of Islam. The Islamic religion was well suited to adapt to different people and cultures as "Islam is a universal faith for all times, all places, and all peoples. It is predicated on the belief that there is but one God, Allah, the Creator of the universe and of humankind,"[29] as explained by Bassiouni. There is a great deal of shared culture across Muslim lands as a result of this shared faith. "Arab Muslim societies and other Muslims have cultural affinities, though every society has preserved its distinguishing characteristics,"[30] states Bassiouni.

Colonialism, communism and the creation of nation states from the nineteenth century, contributed to the destruction of Muslim structures, societies and connections across borders. Where people had previously been linked by huge empires or through religion, this was damaged, destroyed and consequently lost. Professor Akbar S. Ahmed says, "The nineteenth-century European concepts of nationhood created ambiguity and tension among Muslims; nationalism was opposed to the notion of the Ummah. The two were seen as contradictory."[31] Despite the tensions and conflicts caused by nationalism, I have found from personal experience that it is still possible to travel across Muslim lands and find aspects of Islamic cultural familiarity. Travel writer, Tharik Hussain who wrote *Minarets in the Mountains*, echoes this experience in his work where he travelled to the Muslim Balkans and witnessed an existing shared Islamic culture which he immediately found familiar.

As I have endeavoured to highlight, Muslim culture is extremely diverse and full of depth. This is perhaps one of the reasons for its resilience because it has constantly adapted to different surroundings whilst keeping faith at its centre. Muslim culture has had a strong influence on world literature, poetry, architecture, development of languages, cuisine, dress, music and of course, dance. Perhaps this is why it has not easily been destroyed. It has a legacy all over the globe, and also lives within its people through the passing down of traditions within families. The development and contribution of Muslim dance culture to the world is probably the most ignored or lost due to internal conflict within the fold of Islam, as well as the breakdown of Muslim structures due to colonialism. Cultural distortions such as Orientalist interpretations of Muslim dance, have also had a big role to play. These concepts will be explored further.

Lastly, it is important to note that culture is an ever-evolving concept. It is not stagnant. However, even new, evolving forms of culture will have roots in the past, and to understand their development is to understand the people and stories that embody the cultural practice.

4-The Silk Road: Trade, Culture and Dance

The Silk Road, the world's oldest and most historically important trade route and its people, are a core part of this journey of dance. It was this route that enabled such extensive exchanges between communities. It is widely believed to have been the main trade route from 130 BCE until 1453 CE, and the rapid spread of Islam and its accompanying culture through Sufism and trade, can largely be traced along its paths.

This significant network of trade routes, that made up the Silk Road, linked east with west; from China spreading to India, modern-day Pakistan, Afghanistan, and further west to Samarkand, Persia and through to the Mediterranean.

The world was very interconnected even all those years ago. It is hard for us to comprehend, as we think that a global world network is a modern phenomenon due to air travel. But this could not be further from the truth according to Peter Frankopan, who writes extensively about this subject. In antiquity, "the webs of communities wove into each other to create a world that was complex, where tastes and ideas were shaped by products, artistic principles and influences thousands of miles apart."[32]

The Silk Road had a constant flow of trade of exotic items, including precious stones, spices and exciting foods like dates, saffron powder and pistachio nuts. Peaches from Samarkand were considered immensely valuable; they were as large as goose eggs and came to be known in China as golden peaches. The Western world, in particular, was clamouring for these items which were highly sought after and valued in Europe. Spices were particularly popular in Europe, as the exotic spices from the east helped preserve and add flavour to food.

However, goods were not the only treasures to travel the across the Silk Road. As well as trade, there were also cultural, political, and religious interactions between places along the route. "It was not only goods that flowed along the arteries that linked the Pacific, Central Asia, India, the Persian Gulf and the Mediterranean in antiquity; so did ideas... Intellectual and religious exchange had always been animated across this region; now it became more complex and more competitive,"[33] states Frankopan.

The most impactful import to the West was probably the Christian religion which was born in the East. "Christianity has long been associated with the Mediterranean and Western Europe... but in fact every aspect of early Christianity was Asian,"[34] according to Frankopan. This fact often slips people's minds, as the integration of the religion into the Western world has been all-encompassing.

As well as religion, many ideas and types of knowledge were exchanged and transmitted along the route. Art, literature, architecture, painting, music, and dance styles were extensively shared between East and West. Ted Levin, the curatorial director of the Silk Road Project and an associate professor of music at Dartmouth College said, "To this day you find ruptures as well as continuity in the dance styles of India, China, Central Asia... These are the dances of everyday life... The dance movements often represent stylized movements that come from everyday life: animals, ways of working in fields or in herding cultures."[35]

These similarities are even more pronounced in the dances from Muslim cultures along the trade route. There was of course a great deal of interaction between all faiths and cultures due to trade and diplomacy, but the interaction amongst Muslim cultures would have been more common as there was a lot of movement across large Muslim empires for a variety of reasons, including work, trade, intermarriage and Hajj pilgrimage to the Muslim holy site of Mecca. Being of the same faith and speaking the same court languages also lessened barriers to connection.

Muslims travelled immensely; they were traders at heart, following the example of the Prophet Muhammad. When travelling to different Muslim lands, they would encounter similar cultural practices based on the values of Islam. These similarities were seen more obviously in architecture, literature and cuisine, but was, and still is, present in many other cultural expressions.

After the birth of Islam in the seventh century, Muslim empires were gaining more and more land, and quickly. As a result, a large part of the Silk Road fell under the control of the Muslims. Jerusalem was already under the Muslim realm from 637 and remained so for most of the next twelve centuries. There was a break from Muslim rule from 1099 to 1187 CE when Jerusalem was under Christian rule, having been captured by the Crusaders. When Constantinople fell to the Ottomans in 1453, this vital route was now also under Muslim control. Christendom made many attempts through the Crusades, to recapture Jerusalem but only the first one was successful. When European attempts to reach the Holy Land became more and more difficult as a result of the Muslim stronghold of the trade routes, they began to look for another way. This fateful route would be by sea, sailing from the West via the Atlantic. The result was the colonisation of the Americas.

The Muslim control of the Silk Road and their advanced civilisation, meant that Muslim culture would have dominated and shaped the world at this time. This is quite similar to the way the Western world shapes and leads world culture today, although this may once again be changing direction. This Muslim influence would have, and did, reach Europe and the Far East. In Europe, the

Muslims were already ruling Spain from 711 and shaping cultural practices. In fact, the Spanish Muslim legacy lives on in Spain to this day.

Muslim traders had also reached the Far East from as early as the seventh century and Islam began to spread in these regions, including parts of China, Malaysia, Indonesia and the Philippines. As with Spain, the influence of Islamic culture and the religion is very much still alive in these lands.

It is largely due to trade via the Silk Road as well as Sufism that Islam spread so rapidly across the world. This is why the Silk Road is such an important part of the journey of dance in this region. Even before Islam existed, dance was already popular throughout the lands along this ancient trade route. With the advent of Islam, the dance styles were incorporated and influenced by the dominant Muslim culture in which Islamic mystical elements played a big role.

5- Home of Spiritual Dance

The dance of the Sufis or the Muslim brotherhoods is one of the most accepted dance forms in the Muslim world. These are devotional practices and performed in remembrance of God, and are one of the common dance forms found across Islamic lands, as described by Lois Ibsen al-Faruqi. Some may argue that this is not a dance, but if we define dance as a form of movement that expresses inner emotions, then Sufi devotional practices are a perfect fit.

I witnessed a beautiful Sufi gathering in remembrance of God (sema) on my first visit to Istanbul in the 1990s. I remember that this was a time when Turkey was still visibly secular. These Sufi semas were not publicly promoted. We heard about the sema through word of mouth from a family friend, who took us to be part of this spiritual experience. It was deeply moving and something I will never forget.

The most well-known form of Muslim religious dance practice is the dance of the whirling dervishes or the sema.[36] However, this was not the first use of dance for spirituality in Muslim circles. Scholar Annemarie Schimmel points out that, "The Mevlevi tariqa is the only order in which this whirling movement has been institutionalized, though it has been practised throughout the world of Islam from early times."[37]

The Mevlevi Order, that made the Whirling Dervish dance famous, was founded by the son of Jalal ad-Din Rumi, the famous Sufi poet and mystic, in Konya, Anatolia in the thirteenth century and was based on his father's teachings. Rumi, the great Muslim poet and mystic, is integral to the story of this dance form. He is very popular all over the world, including in the West. I've noticed that in some mainstream works on Rumi, the connection to his faith is not obvious. As a result of this, there is some ignorance about Rumi's religion and love for God, which inspired his works. Understanding this connection is necessary to really unravel the depth of Rumi's teachings.

Rumi was born in 1207 in Balkh, present-day Afghanistan, but his family was forced to flee to Damascus and then Konya (present-day Turkey) due to the threat of the Mongol invasion. He started off as a very knowledgeable and orthodox religious leader. However, after meeting and being mentored by the wandering dervish, Shams of Tabriz, Rumi was transformed into the great spiritual leader and poet whom we know today. The influence of Rumi's teachings spread rapidly across the Muslim world and beyond. In his poetry, Rumi expresses deep love of God and routinely uses music and dance imagery to communicate the "inner song of his soul."[38]

The Mevlevis, in remembrance of God, subsequently created this beautiful synchronised and mystical whirling dance form. However, it was not born out of a desire to be aesthetically pleasing, but the result of mystical ecstasy.

The sema is a dhikr or 'remembrance' of God, and can take the form of dance as well. It is a seven-part ceremony and each step of the ritual has a deep meaning and significance. It is practised to music with a melodious ney flute or drums, oud (short neck lute), rebab (stringed instrument) and sometimes just the human voice. The sounds represents breath, which is of course fundamental to life. All the dervishes begin by sitting in a row, then rise slowly and move to greet their 'shaykh' or 'master'. The dervish wears a tall, conical headdress that is supposed to symbolise the ego's tombstone and the white skirt that is the ego's shroud. They wear a black cloak which is removed in the ceremony, signifying the rebirth and connection to the truth and one's inner purpose.

The dervish begins the movements with his or her arms crossed over each other against the chest, fingers gripping the opposite shoulder. In this way their body form resembles an alif (first letter of the Arabic alphabet) or number one, and is symbolic of the Oneness of God. The arms only open out once the dervish has built up momentum and made two or three turns. The ceremony is profoundly beautiful, and full of depth and connection, and the dervishes are thought to be a channel to God's blessings.

When the dervish is whirling with arms held out, the right hand faces the heavens (although this can vary), to receive God's Benevolence and they look towards their left hand which is facing the ground, to symbolise that they are passing God's blessings and spiritual gifts to those in the audience. Of the four periods in which they turn (called salaams), the first three require them to not only turn on their own axis, but to also move in an anti-clockwise direction around the circle in which they are performing. Only in the final, fourth section do they whirl on the spot and keep their position. The choreography can be quite complex.

As the dervish is going through the rituals, their voices chant 'Allah' or 'God' inwardly and silently, and the repetition of movement and chanting gets faster and faster. The ideal goal, through the movements, is to lead to the complete stripping of the ego, and culminate in a spiritual high or perfection known as 'fanafillah', which is a state of enlightenment. The sema is about complete submission to God, and the annihilation of the self. However, this ideal state of enlightenment needs a lot of work, and sometimes it is more of a mild experience rather than a full-blown one. Whirling is about becoming exceptionally present and aware.

The whirling dervish ritual appears as a breath-taking dance ceremony, but is so much more. It is the beautiful flowing movement combined with prayer, meditation and enlightenment. Schimmel points out that the whirling movement has a long-standing connection with spirituality across the world, even before Islam. "In fact, dancing and whirling belong to the oldest and religious acts of all... In primitive societies, dance had a magical character - rituals to produce rain or ensure victory were usually connected with dance."[39]

Schimmel states that although the sema is classed as a religious act in Sufi Muslim circles, it has had its fair share of controversy in the Muslim world. "The problem of sema, 'hearing' was a major cause of differences among the schools. There were complicated problems as to whether 'listening to music' and 'dancing movement' are genuine utterances of mystical states or illegitimate attempts to gain, by one's own effort, a state that can only be granted by God; the views of the authorities are clearly divided."[40] This has been a consistent debate in the history of Islam.

Iranian philosopher, Seyyed Hossein Nasr, states that this controversy has always existed about the validity of music and dance in Islam. He explains, in an interview with singer Sami Yusuf, that "Ghazali says, 'If there is in the soul, a love for God, for the truth, for heavenly beauty, music intensifies it... if there is only love of the world, of worldly passions, it intensifies that.'"[41]

In a very interesting view, Seyyed Hossein Nasr implies that this diversity in his opinion is natural, and perhaps an intentional act of God. The validity of the act of music and dance is dependent on the state of one's own heart. There are some music and dance forms that uplift the soul and some that destroy it. Nasr says, "That's why the whole question of halal and haram and music in Islam is so complicated, why it was never banned by all the ulema and never agreed upon by all the ulema."[42] The music that is used in the sema is intended to have a spiritual purpose. He adds, music is, "surely the most eloquent way of expressing the deepest truth of Islam, and especially today, it plays a very important role."[43]

Spiritual music and dance has historically played a huge role in bringing people into the fold of Islam and contributed to large-scale conversions in the Muslim world. Even now, these cultural traditions inspire interest from non-Muslim audiences. Schimmel writes, "It was the musical side of some of the fraternities that attracted large masses. Those who longed for an emotional kind of worship that ritual prayer could not really provide might find it by listening to music or by participating in the dance movement."[44]

The spread of Islam, across all corners of the world, has also been attributable to the brotherhoods and the spiritual connection to God. "The orders were adaptable to every social level as well as to the several races represented in Islam... It is a well-established fact that large parts of India,

Indonesia, and Black Africa were Islamicized by the untiring activity of Sufi preachers who manifested in their lives the basic obligations of Islam, simple love of and trust in God, and love of the Prophet and their fellow creatures, without indulging in logical or juridical hairsplitting,"[45] states Schimmel.

Rumi's impact on Central Asian, Persian-Turkish culture was immense. This influence extended naturally to India, where the Mughal rulers of similar heritage, promoted this same culture and spirituality. Schimmel observes, "The Islamization of the country was achieved largely by the preaching of the dervishes, not by the sword."[46] It has been said that the role of mysticism in India contributed massively to the spread of Islam.

The influence remains, to this day, in both modern-day India and Pakistan with the veneration of Sufi saints. It has also penetrated the culture in these countries through poetry, literature, music and dance forms. Well-loved twentieth century Urdu and Persian poet, Muhammad Iqbal, utilised a great deal of Sufi imagery in his work, as did other poets. They may not have always subscribed to the highest levels of Sufism, but the imagery they used was a universal poetic language. In Iqbal's poetry, "His imagery, like that a great deal of most Turkish, Persian, or Urdu poets, is largely coloured by Sufi symbolism: as much as he detested the kind of enthralling, 'otherworldly'" mysticism that he thought was hidden behind Hafiz's beautiful verses, he himself used the whole fabric of Sufi imagery in his poetry, though he often re-interpreted it,"[47] according to Schimmel.

Iqbal and other Sufi poets have had their poetry turned into music and consequently dance, and this has happened all over the Muslim world. The movements that are performed are inspired by the words of the poem, and display the same spiritual essence that is present in the content of the poetry.

In Pakistan, the Sufi dance form is called 'dhamal'. It is an energetic whirling movement, and symbolises the spiritual ecstasy of the dancer. It is accompanied by a characteristic Pakistani drum. Both men and women take part in this dance ritual, and it has created much controversy amongst certain orthodox elements of the Pakistani society. Amjad Sabri, the famous Pakistani Sufi Qawwali singer, was tragically shot dead in 2016 by two gunmen who believed he was going against Islam. Such acts of callous murder show to what lengths some people can go to when they are convinced that their interpretation of religion is the only truth.

In other parts of the world, such as in the Ottoman Empire, Sufism, in particular the Mevlevi dervishes, were very popular and exerted great influence in society as well as with the elite. However, they were targeted not by extreme religious groups in this case, but by secular leaders. The Sufis in general were felt to have had too much power and influence on Turkish people, and in 1925, Mustafa Kemal Ataturk, the father of modern Turkey, issued a blanket ban. Ataturk wanted to create a Westernised and secular Turkey, as opposed to the Islamic model which had been dominant in the Ottoman Empire. Ataturk, and others at the time, believed Westernisation was the path to modernisation and financial prosperity. According to Bruce Miller in his book, *Rumi Comes to America*, "Ataturk was quite clear, 'Turkey is a modern country that has no time for dervish magic.'"[48]

At face value it seems like Ataturk disliked Sufis; interestingly, however, there is an alternative view that argues Ataturk was actually a Mevlevi. Miller states, "Despite the draconian decrees, Ataturk may have been sympathetic and even aligned with the Mevlevis. He reportedly stated to the head of the Mevlevi, 'You have made a great difference in combating ignorance and religious fanaticism for centuries, as well as making contributions to science and the arts. However, we are obliged not to make any exceptions and must include Mevlevi tekkes (in the ban). Nonetheless, the ideas and teachings of Rumi will not only exist forever, but they will emerge even more powerfully in the future.'"[49]

In the 1950s, the Turkish government eased restrictions on the whirling dervish ceremony, and it was again allowed to be performed in public. In fact, it established an educational-cultural foundation which is linked to the Turkish Ministry of Culture and Tourism, ensuring its survival. The sema is allowed to be performed as a cultural symbol but not as a religious ceremony.

As a spiritual dance form, the whirling dervish ceremony has had such a huge impact on the Islamic and Western culture across the world. It attracts audiences of all backgrounds to observe its beauty. As the dance intends to appeal to the soul and the connection with one's creator, it transcends all boundaries, which is perhaps its purpose.

In 2008, the Mevlevi sema ceremony was recognised by UNESCO as amongst the Masterpieces of the Oral and Intangible Heritage of Humanity. There are also other forms of Sufi dance.

BEKTASHI DANCE

The Bektashis are a Sufi order in Turkey who follow the teachings of Hajji Bektash Veli. There are a large number of Bektashis in Albania, and in some parts of Eastern Europe. The most famous Bektashi was Yunus Emre (c.1238-c.1320) who lived around the same time as Rumi. He was a shepherd who wrote poems in Turkish (whereas Rumi wrote in Persian, primarily). Turks consider Yunus Emre the father of Turkish poetry. The folk dances of the Bektashis usually involve both men and women, and sometimes these incorporate mixed-sex partner dancing.

SUFI HADRA

The hadra, which means 'presence' in Arabic, is another Sufi dance ritual practised by many Sufi orders in Africa and some other areas around the Silk Road such as Central Asia, parts of the Middle East and Turkey. It is a dhikr or devotional practice; the words recited alongside the movement are in praise of God and the Prophet Muhammad. The movement that the words inspire, is deeply rhythmic as well as energetic, and can be mesmerising to behold. Women also perform their own hadra, though these are almost never filmed.

SHASHMAQAM

Shashmaqam is a spiritual music and dance style connected to Central Asia. It is popular and deeply rooted to Sufism and the sema traditions. See Chapter 10 for more details on shashmaqam.

The following chapters will explore the different dance forms found in the Muslim world, as we journey from East to West along the ancient Silk Road.

6- Dance Legacy of Islamic Spain

Muslims ruled Spain for eight centuries. The first Muslim rulers were a diverse ethnic group, including Berbers from North Africa and Arabs. They became known as Moors. They defeated the crumbling rule of the Visigoths in 711. The last stronghold of the Muslim Empire in Spain was Granada, and it fell to Catholic rulers, Ferdinand of Aragon and Isabelle of Castille in 1492. Muslims and Jews were driven out of Spain or forced to convert to Christianity.

Eight hundred years of Muslim rule was an extensive time to embed the Islamic faith and culture. During this time Spain became a highly advanced civilisation. Some of the greatest philosophers the world has known were from Muslim Spain, including Averroes (Ibn Rushd), Maimonides and Ibn Arabi. Their works have immensely influenced European culture and society, but their contribution to the world's learning and advancement is not as pronounced as it should be, and in some places entirely written out of history.

These great thinkers were responsible for translating ancient Greek philosophical works into Arabic, which subsequently made their way into the European lingua franca, making it accessible for Europeans to read Plato and Aristotle. Author, Jason Webster, states, "This learning laid the groundwork for the 'later' rebirth of Europe."[50]

The obvious Muslim legacy in Spain is of course the magnificent Alhambra Palace in Granada, built by the Nasrid dynasty in the fourteenth century. The Great Mosque in Cordoba, built by ruler Abd al-Rahman I in the late eighth century, is another reminder of this great Muslim past. However, it would be wrong to ignore all the other plentiful reminders of Muslim rule across Spain that are more subtle yet deeply embedded.

The Muslims, "Not only brought with them their religion but many aspects of their vibrant culture that undoubtedly influenced local customs still in effect today. Their long and powerful presence infiltrated and formed many aspects of Andalusi culture such as the arts, architecture, literature, cuisine, sciences, poetry, dance and music,"[51] states author Ana Ruiz.

The Spanish language itself contains a multitude of words originating from Arabic; it is believed that fifteen percent of Spanish comes from Arabic. There was also a great deal of intermarriage among the Muslims and native Spanish people; as a result, the DNA of Spanish people is very mixed, and Islamic customs and culture are part and parcel of everyday life. In his book *Andalus: Unlocking the Secrets of Moorish Spain*, Webster states, in a tongue-in-cheek way that Spain is still a Moorish country but hidden behind a Spanish Catholic exterior. He infers that the Moorish presence is still all around if one observes closely with open eyes. Webster says that the Muslim presence in Spain is, "A cultural phenomenon, where Spain, intellectually, artistically, religiously and commercially, became part of the Islamic sphere of influence."[52]

The Muslims that were left in Spain after the fall of Granada in 1492, were either forcibly converted to Christianity through the Spanish Inquisition or forced to leave, as were the Jews, many of of the latter were given sanctuary by the Ottoman Empire. Many Muslims actually stayed and practised their religion in secret, passing on customs and traditions through generations. From the time of the Inquisition, Spanish rulers tried their best to rid the country of any Islamic presence. However, the Muslim legacy has lived on and this is mainly due to the mixed heritage of the people, and the huge influence the faith and culture exerted on the country over eight hundred years of rule.

The Moors have left an imprint on educational institutions and libraries, as learning was integral to Islam. The oldest university in the world (which is still active) was founded by a Muslim woman named Fatima al-Fihri in Fez, Morocco. Some of the oldest universities in Europe were established in Andalusia. There is still a presence of public baths or hammams due to the integral aspect of hygiene in Islam, beautiful courtyards and gardens, another well-known legacy of Muslims across the world, and of course, architecture.

The father of Spanish literature, Cervantes, is said to have based aspects of his famous book *Don Quixote* on Moorish figures and culture. He was, after all, writing at a time when Moorish rule in Spain was a not too distant memory.

The impact of Muslim culture extends to Spanish music and dance, the most well-known being flamenco. The Muslims rulers integrated their own traditions with those already existing in Spain; perhaps that was one of the reasons that they had such a lasting impact, because they were already rooted in local practices. Ruiz says, "The Moors occupying this land for eight centuries greatly influenced the music of Southern Spain - as you can distinctively hear its Arabic influence."[53]

The music of flamenco has a striking similarity to music in North Africa. It is commonly believed to be a beautiful combination of Romani and Moorish traditions, and arose at a time when these communities were living closely together after the Inquisition, and when Muslims were practising their religion and culture secretly in the underground scene. Ruiz states, "The meeting of cante gitano (gypsy song) and Andalusian folk music as early as the 16th century seems to have been the starting point that would, very gradually, led to the development of flamenco."[54]

The Romani travellers came to Spain in the twelfth century from what is now modern-day India and Pakistan, and found comfort among the Andalusian culture, having come from an Eastern tradition as well. Ruiz says, "When the Gypsies arrived in Andalusia, their Hindi musical system and dance styles fused well with the local Andalusian and Arabic influences."[55]

The Romanis were influenced by the kathak dance styles being practised in India, as well as more specific Muslim dance forms, based on Central Asian,

Persian and Turkish culture, as North India was ruled by Muslim empires at this time. "Kathak and Flamenco have somewhat similar leg positioning, raised elbows, and rhythmic patterns, along with fast turns and sharp, angular body positions, and arm movements. Graceful movements of the hands are similar as both cultures use splayed finger and curved positions that trace circular motions in the air. The imaginary circles are called floreos or 'flowerings' of the hand,"[56] according to Ruiz.

The flamenco also has elements of Moorish zambra dance. Writer, Medina Tenour Whiteman says, "The zambra style of flamenco dance, performed at gypsy weddings, evolved from older Moorish styles and has many similarities to belly dancing. The word 'zambra' in Moroccan Arabic simply means 'party'."[57]

The Moorish zambras included dancers holding hands with each other, and was said to have been danced to, "Wind instruments of the sounds of pipes and flutes,"[58] states Ruiz. It is even believed, by some, that these dances influenced Morris dancing, hence the name being similar to Moors, the name for Muslims. Ruiz adds, "By the fifteenth century, the dance of the Moriscos spread throughout Europe and particularly to Great Britain where many believed it evolved into the Morris Dance."[59]

The other obvious connection to the Moors is the chant of 'ole' used during the flamenco dance as praise. This actually comes from the Arabic word 'wa'Allah' or 'by Allah', and was used during poetry recitals, as a way of showing appreciation. According to Ruiz, "The tradition of palmas and encouraging a performer by shouting words of praise (such as ole, from the Arabic expression wa'Allah, meaning 'by God!') in Flamenco goes back to the Zambras of the Moriscos."[60]

The connection of flamenco to the Muslim world is even apparent through the musical instruments used to play the accompanying songs. "The first contribution that Muslims might be said to have made to flamenco is simply providing the guitar,"[61] says Whiteman. The guitar was born out of Spain as a result of the influence of Islamic instruments and music. Ziryab, a well-known Kurdish[62] musician, composer and cultural ambassador arrived in Andalusia from Baghdad in the ninth century. In 822, he established the first music school in Cordoba. He would often be playing the lute, and "His innovative ideas inspired him to modify the lute by adding a fifth bass string; this instrument evolved into the Spanish guitar."[63] states Ruiz.

The legacy of the Moors is sadly skimmed over in mainstream history, which relegates this impactful era to a footnote in Spain's past. It is seen as fringe history rather than world history. However, the Muslim legacy in Spain is still strong and in some ways glaringly obvious, especially in the south where I have visited many times. Ruiz says, "Many cultures shaped Andalusia but it was the Muslims who left the strongest imprint, particularly in architecture, making it distinct from any other region in Europe."[64]

7-Ottoman History and Dance Evolution

Turkey, once the centre of the Ottoman Empire, was the beacon of the Islamic world until the nineteenth century. Despite the dismantling of the Empire, modern-day Turkey is fused with an abundance of tradition and culture, and the presence of what was once the focal point of a mighty superpower, can be felt.

I have travelled to Turkey many times, the first time was when I was a teenager with my family. The main thing that strikes me every time I visit is the remnants of grandeur and centuries of tradition; from beautiful majestic mosques, unparalleled architecture, bazaars with exotic goods, to the aroma of Turkish coffee and freshly made baklava.

When I first visited in the 1990s, it felt very much a secular country. However, in my subsequent visits, I noticed a stronger expression of Muslim identity. This visible 'Muslimness' is a growing movement in the country. Very recently, the Hagia Sophia, which was a Byzantine cathedral turned mosque in 1453, and then converted into a museum in 1934, was turned back into a mosque in 2020 under the leadership of President Erdogan.

Despite the nationalist movement in the early twentieth century led by Kemal Ataturk, which tried to break from the Ottoman past and modernise the country along Western lines, the legacy of the Ottomans and the Muslim faith and culture still lives on. The history and mysticism of this land oozes from its very fabric, and you can still observe traditional Sufi dhikr ceremonies. Sufi lodges (tekkes) were closed down in the early 1900s by Ataturk and are still officially banned. However, spiritual dance practices can still take place privately, or even publicly as long as they're presented as historical re-enactments for tourism and cultural events, rather than religious practice.

The centre of the Ottoman Empire was strategic as it borders many sea and trade routes, and was a significant stop on the Silk Road. As a result, there is a diversity of people and heritage in this historic land. Some passed through; many remained. The Ottomans went on to rule a vast area of the world, from northern Europe to parts of Asia and the Middle East. This resulted in a mixing of cultures and traditions, which have their own distinct practices but have also influenced each other throughout the course of history. Consequently, there is a huge array of folk dances which are varied and diverse.

The Ottoman Sultans, whilst adopting other cultures into their Empire, also unified the lands under their rule into a common Ottoman culture and tradition. As historian Suraiya Faroqhi says, "The Ottoman Empire was a state of many peoples. A variety of Christian and Muslim inhabitants of the Balkans were subjects of the Sultan, and the same thing applied to the largely Muslim, Arabic-speaking inhabitants of Syria, Egypt and Iraq. Although the upper classes of these groups participated to a greater or lesser extent in Ottoman high culture, regional cultures remained very varied."[65]

There are very few sources about dance in the Ottoman Empire. There are some images we can obtain from Ottoman miniatures, but the early dances seem to be hard to identify. The missing information coincides with the orthodox views towards dance within traditional Muslim societies, which is perhaps why it was not recorded. However, this could also have been because dance was not generally a documented history, but a living and evolving practice, passed on through generations.

OTTOMAN HISTORY

Ottoman history and cultural norms would have shaped the way dance developed and evolved across the Empire over time. We know that dance reflects the essence of the people and their stories, therefore learning more about this can help to create a picture of what would have influenced dance at this time.

What we know is that the Ottoman Empire was founded by Osman I, who was a nomadic Turkmen chief, and it is his descendants that ruled for six hundred years, from the 1300s until 1922 when the Empire was dissolved. Osman had a significant dream one night when staying at the home of a Sufi religious leader, Sheikh Edebali. He saw a tree growing from his navel, and it flourished and spread all over the world. This was said to be a prophecy that his descendants were to be great rulers. Sufism was a big part of the Ottoman rulers' culture right from the very beginning, and the Islamic scholars who advised the Sultans were also schooled in the Sufi tradition.

Osman's descendants fought against the Byzantines and the Mongols, and were soon to become a major Muslim rival to Byzantium, the centre of Christianity at the time. The Empire grew further under Osman's successors Orhan (1324-1360) and Murad I (1360-1389). Murad I expanded the Ottoman territory to much of the Balkans including Macedonia, Bulgaria and Serbia. Beyazid I, his successor, expanded further into Eastern Europe where much of the legacy is still alive even to this day. The Balkans had over six hundred years of Ottoman rule, and even now there is much Ottoman Muslim heritage embedded in the land. There are Ottoman-built mosques and architecture, some attributed to the Chief Ottoman architect Mimar Sinan who lived in the sixteenth century. The names of places, people, cuisines and cultural norms, such as hospitality and welcoming travellers, are from the Ottomans' Islamic faith. Much of this part of Europe is still Muslim and has been for several hundred years. There is also a rich Sufi heritage in the Balkans, another legacy of the Ottomans. The following chapter will further explore the Balkans.

To further expand the growing power of the Ottomans, Sultan Mehmed II (1451-1481) conquered the Byzantine capital of Constantinople in 1453, now known as Istanbul. This was a major breakthrough for the Ottomans, but devastating for Christendom. The power dynamic was beginning to change, and the Ottoman Empire was becoming a force to be reckoned with.

Following Mehmed II's reign, the Empire went from strength to strength and expanded into central Europe and the Middle East. As the Ottomans started to rule a larger area, they exerted influence on the culture of these new lands, but also adopted new cultures into their fold. Even to this day, there is a diversity of cultural traditions, with elements of shared practices.

Bayezid II (1481-1512) opened up the Empire to the Jews who had been forced out of Spain due to the Inquisition. Many Jews came to the Ottoman Empire and enjoyed relative peace and protection. The Empire was a multicultural and multi-faith melting pot, and the Jewish community settled here for hundreds of years. They also brought with them their own traditions, further enhancing local practices.

Sultan Selim I (1512-20) was able to conquer the Arab lands from the Mamluks, and this included the most holy sites of Islam in Mecca and Medina. This gave the Ottomans a stronger standing in the Muslim community and they became seen as the leaders of all Muslims across the world. The conquest of the Middle Eastern region also gave the Ottomans direct control of the Silk Road trade route between Europe and East Asia.

Selim was succeeded by his son Suleyman, who ruled from 1520-66. He was called the 'Magnificent' in Europe and 'Kanuni' or 'Lawgiver' by the Ottomans. His reign was seen as the golden age of Ottoman history when the Empire was at its peak. Suleyman had his eyes set on Hungary and took Belgrade in 1521. Suleyman also robustly dealt with the Knights of the Order of St. John at Rhodes, who for two hundred years were targeting trade through Ottoman territories as well as threatening the safety of Muslim pilgrims to Mecca. The Knights were driven out of Rhodes in 1523, and re-established themselves ten years later in Malta.

The Ottomans were by no means perfect or practising Muslims. However, they were driven by Sufi ideals of Islam and were keen to be seen as the leaders of all the Muslim world, especially after conquering the holy sites of Islam in Mecca and Medina.

With the growing power of the European nations from the eighteenth century and the modernisation and scientific advancement of the Western world, the tide of power began to slowly change. Where once the Muslim empires were global powers, their strength now started to decline. It is believed that Western influence on the Ottoman Empire took place from the early eighteenth century, known in Ottoman history as the 'Tulip Period' (1717-1730). The sultan at the time was Ahmed III. This is also the period when the tulip, as a symbol of the Ottomans, emerged and became closely linked to the culture and the people.

Western Europe was becoming increasingly commercially adept while the opposite was happening for the Ottomans. This resulted in a reversal of roles, and the Ottomans now wanted to follow in the footsteps of Western empires. This imitation extended to arts and culture as well. Architectural developments, instead of only looking eastwards for inspiration, started to incorporate European baroque style, and mimicking French palace design. Clothing was copied from European fashions, and court life also began to mirror the European norms. The Turkish printing press began mass producing works for the first time in the eighteenth century, which was a slow start compared to the rest of Europe. Military reforms were slowly implemented based on the advanced Western model.

Sultan Selim III (1789-1807) rapidly continued the modernisation and reforms of the Empire into his reign, and encouraged them to flourish. He is often referred to as the ruler behind modern reforms. From this period onwards, the Westernisation of the Empire only increased. This coincided with more unpleasant changes for the Ottomans as they began to lose control of regions under their rule, as the trend moved towards establishing independent nation states.

The Tanzimat Reforms followed in the nineteenth century (1839-1876), which was a concerted effort to bring the Ottoman Empire on an equal footing with Western European nations. The legal reforms tried to separate politics and governance from religion, and moved towards secularisation. This was obviously not welcomed by religious leaders, and others who had a vested interest in the old system, such as the Ottoman elite military corp or the Janissaries.[66]

INFLUENCE OF EUROPEAN DANCE

As the Ottoman Empire was becoming more Westernised and looking to Europe for inspiration, classical European dance began to grow and flourish.

Empires started to split up, dissolve and develop into nation states. This new identity required a unifying narrative. Newly-formed states were trying to establish themselves and forge a unique culture and identity, and dance was one of the ways to achieve this.

In Turkey, "The discovery of dance as a symbol of national identity came in the early 1900s with the writings of Riza Tefvik and Selim Siri Tarcan. Coming from the 'Young Turk' tradition, these writers established a more direct relationship between folk dances and national identity,"[67] according to historian Arzu Ozturkmen.

Selim Siri Tarcan was a Turkish educator and politician, and part of the movement to bring Western dance to the nation. His daughter, Selma Selim Sim, was also a proponent of using dance for the purposes of forging a strong national identity. Ozturkmen states, "Both father and daughter saw in dance an opportunity to look 'more Western' and acknowledged the importance of placing women at the center of the dance space - in schools and on stage - to further enhance this Western image."[68]

Turkey began to establish opera houses and ballet schools. Women, who traditionally were not seen to perform in public, also began to take their positions in this newly emerging dance arena. There was also a desire to use traditional folk dances, merged with European classical dance styles, in order to create a dance form unique to Turkey; a combination of traditional and Western elements. Ozturkmen says, "It was the idea of the Minister of Cultural Affairs that the state-sponsored ballet dancers should learn 'our national rhythms'! The following day's newspapers gave a broad coverage to the event displaying on their front page, ballerinas crying in shock, despair and humiliation."[69]

Before operation nationalism, folk dances existed for millennia in their local regions connected to ancient traditions, the landscape, natural environment, and with the advent of Islam, a Sufi-style spiritual connection to the Creator. Although the dance had similarities to neighbouring lands and dance styles were shared along the Silk Road, they were not uniform or used for mass public performance.

With Turkish nationalism, folk dances were taken out of rural areas, shaped and controlled to fit the emerging nation's narrative. This began in 1932 with the founding of the 'People's Houses', which was a network of village and small-town institutions that started to collect information on the local dances. "Following the disintegration of the Ottoman Empire and the formation of the Turkish Republic in 1923, the state started a research program to revive the Central Asian roots and Anatolian folklore. Turkish nationalism, like all other nationalisms, needed to construct its national cultural symbols and disseminate them within the popular strata,"[70] according to Ozturkmen.

The Turkish nationalists wanted to move away from the country's Ottoman-Muslim past, and steer the new identity towards a more Westernised ideal. They wanted to recreate history and mould it to suit their secular intentions. "The Republican ideology wanted to mediate and standardise in Turkey: a secular and 'modernised' image of the Turkish nation, as opposed to the traditional Muslim-Ottoman identity,"[71] states Ozturkmen.

Alongside the process of standardising folk dances, there was also a drive to support and create modern European forms of dance. Dame Ninette de Valois, an Irish-born British dancer, opened the first official ballet school in Istanbul in 1948. This led to the creation of the Turkish State Ballet. Ozturkmen says, "State Ballet Ensemble had always had an agenda to 'synthesise' the West with the East and tradition with modernity."[72]

BELLY DANCING

Belly dancing is a common style across the Middle East, Iran and the Ottoman territories. However, as with Middle Eastern belly dance, the Turkish belly dance that we see today is not what was usually practised in the Ottoman courts.

The root of influence on traditional Turkish belly dance is from the Middle East, but also has Romani influences as well. The dance was not as provocative in the Ottoman courts as it is today, and it was mainly performed by boy dancers (kocekler). "This dance is hardly favoured in Turkey and certainly a dance in the Imperial Serail (Harem) never takes a provocative, lascivious or indecent form which the Westerners imagine it to have and which can be seen performed in their own countries by dancers more or less Oriental. The actual belly dance is really a dance of Arabic origin,"[73] according to historian, Leyla Hammefendi.

Many of the English-speaking accounts of Ottoman culture in the eighteenth century, including dance, came from Lady Mary Wortley Montagu, who travelled to the Ottoman Empire with her husband, a politician and British Ambassador to Constantinople. They were both welcomed into the upper echelons of Ottoman society; she also learnt to speak Turkish and had a desire to learn Arabic. Lady Mary absorbed a great deal and learnt much from the advanced Ottomans, which she took back to England with her. One of the ground-breaking discoveries she is recognised for is promoting the use of the smallpox inoculation in England, which she discovered in the Ottoman Empire, as it had treated the disease successfully.

Lady Mary did not describe the dance she witnessed in the Ottoman Courts to be as sexualised as it is now. In a letter in 1718, she wrote, "This dance was very different from what I had seen before. Nothing could be more artful, or more proper to raise certain ideas. The tunes so soft!–the motions so languishing!–accompanied with pauses and dying eyes! half-falling back, and then recovering themselves in so artful a manner."[74]

RELIGIOUS DANCE

Alongside folk dances and court dances within the Ottoman Empire, religious dance also thrived. This was a more acceptable form of dance in the eyes of the orthodoxy, although it still raised concerns and caused its fair share of controversy. Ozturkmen says, "Religious movement systems, often referred to as 'religious dance,' were widely performed around the empire as part of larger rituals. The sema of the Alevi Muslim communities, for example, was usually performed as part of the cem ritual in village contexts. Many religious orders (tarikats) also performed their whirling rituals (sema ayini) in different towns and cities around the empire."[75]

The most well known of the religious Sufi dance practices is the dance of the Mevlevi Dervishes or Whirling Dervishes. This is called the sema and is part of a wider spiritual ceremony including dhikr or praise in remembrance of God and the Prophet Muhammad. The sema and other Sufi dance rituals started to mix with pre-Islamic folk dance styles. However, the meaning and story of the dance began to change, from perhaps worshipping or venerating nature and the environment, to reverence for God who created these elements. The main way we can see the Sufi influence on folk dance forms is through the language of the sung poetry that accompany the movements, which often come from the works of revered Sufi saints.

Ironically, while the Ottomans began to look towards the west for dance inspiration and validation, Western dancers were fascinated with the 'dances' of the Orient, and in particular the Sufi whirling dervish religious ceremony. Theodore Barber says, "Western dancers for many years had been looking to the Orient as a source of inspiration, and in the 1920s their attention was called to the spinning of the Mevlevis as a hitherto relatively unexplored dance form."[76]

Sadly, in the West, often the spiritual context of the Sufi dance was removed. The Muslim imagery on the sets, costumes, and mimicking of the movements remained, but the dances were in fact a visual fantasy of the Western imagination and thoughts about the East. "(Jean) Borlin apparently gave the dance an orgiastic interpretation, in keeping with the general public's conception of the Orient,"[77] states Barber. It is important to note, however, that there are some authentic expressions of Sufi dance which have made their way to the Unites States and other parts of the Western world.

POPULAR FOLK DANCES IN TURKEY

HALAY

Halay is known as the national dance of Turkey and is danced mainly on happy occasions such as weddings. Although it may have different variations according to where it is danced, the general formation is to form a circle in a type of line-dance fashion. More commonly, dancers hold each other's hands, fingers or shoulders, and the first and last in the formation wave a piece of cloth. The instruments which are normally used for the halay are wind instruments, such as the 'zurna' and traditional drums - the 'davul.'

• Whirling Dervishes, Istanbul

ZEYBEK

Zeybek is a popular dance of Western Turkey. There are over 150 dance styles of zeybek varying from region and tempo. It is mainly a male dance, but there is a growing trend of females also participating in this dance. The dancers stroll around in a circle, and one knee bends to touch the ground. The arms are held out to the sides and they snap their fingers. The Greek Zeybekiko dance descends from this Turkish dance.

Selim Siri Tarcan went to Sweden to learn how to choreograph folk dances and brought the knowledge back home. However, this did not take off in Turkey with the zeybek. Historian, Anthony Shay says, "In 1916, he choreographed the zeybek–which he called Tarcan zeybeği–to appeal to a sophisticated urban Turkish audience. However, the modernization of the zeybek dance was never fully embraced in Turkey because of the nationalistic and ethnic appeal that staged traditional folk dances had for Turkish audiences."[78]

KILIK KALCAN

The history of the Kilik Kalcan folk dance goes back to 1326 and the conquest of Bursa by the Ottomans. It is a military style dance; it is not meant to promote hostility but is in fact a dance for peace. The dance is now over seven hundred years old and is not performed to music, which is rare, but the drama of the dance and the sounds of the swords and shields are sufficient to signify the impact of the movements.

An article via Anadalou Agency states, "Kılıç-kalkan, a folk dance performed since the fourteenth century, emerged following a battlefield victory. Although the dance is performed with symbolic swords and shields, its choreography has emphasized brotherhood and peace for seven centuries"[79] The dancers go through the motions of the battlefield, but in the end they embrace, realising that peace is better than war. The dance was formalised and choreographed in the early 1900s, and it is this set piece that is normally learned, taught and performed to promote Turkey's heritage.

8-The Balkans–Muslim Europe

INFLUENCE OF THE OTTOMAN EMPIRE ON BALKAN CULTURE

The Bosnian Muslim connection is known by most people, mainly due to the tragic genocide which took place in the 1990s. I was a young child at the time, but remember this tragic period well. I knew there were white Muslims because I had grown up with family and friends from diverse communities. However, it was only as I got older, I began to properly understand the extent of Muslim history and heritage in Europe, and realise that Islam is in fact indigenous to Europe.

The genocide highlighted there were Muslims in Bosnia, but there are also Muslims living across Europe, including the Balkans, and have been for centuries. The predominant cultural influence on Muslim communities in the Balkans is from the Ottoman Empire, which began to establish its rule from the fourteenth to fifteenth centuries. It is important to note though that there was Muslim presence in this region even before this time through various other Muslim tribes and people. The Ottoman influence has been the most prominent, however. It lasted consistently for over six hundred years, and is still alive and thriving, to this day despite various attempts to eradicate it.

While the Balkan states were fighting amongst themselves, the Ottomans took control of Adrianople (now Edirne in Turkey) in 1326, which gave them the base to make inroads further into the Balkans. It was a slow process that took more than a hundred years with Serbia falling first in 1389 at the Battle of Kosovo, Bulgaria in 1396, Bosnia in 1463, Herzegovina in 1482 and Montenegro in 1499.

In the Balkan lands which the Ottomans went on to rule, they brought with them their own administrative and bureaucratic systems. They also appointed their own governors, although many local rulers converted to Islam and remained in position.

Local people were not forced to convert when the Ottomans arrived, this was standard practice within the Empire. Some historians believe that the 'jizya' tax applied to non-Muslim subjects was the main reason not to force conversion. However, there are other historical views that point out coercion was not a sensible way of enabling sustainable rule, as it would cause too much discontentment and strife. The Qur'an also explicitly says, "There shall be no coercion in matters of faith."[80] This has surely had a decisive influence on enlightened Muslim rulers. The Ottomans were practical, and proud to rule over diverse people and faiths. In his book 'Minarets in the Mountains: A Journey into Muslim Europe' Tharik Hussain says, "This Ottoman tolerance for other faiths was highly unusual in pre-Enlightenment Europe, but quite normal in Muslim Europe."[81] In fact, the Jews that were expelled via the Inquisition in Spain were given sanctuary within Ottoman lands including Eastern Europe.

There are many beautiful stories of religious coexistence in the Balkans, but a story close to my heart is the story that Hussain tells of Bosnian Muslim scholar and librarian, Dervis Korkut (1888-1969). He was the man who saved the Sarajevo Haggadah from being stolen by the Nazis. This Haggadah is one of the world's oldest Sephardic Haggadahs; a stunning bound manuscript with illuminated gold and silver leaf that tells a story of the Jewish exodus from Egypt. Korkut also saved Mira Papo, a Jewish girl, from the Nazis by bringing her into his family and hiding her true identity. Hussain says, "As far back as 1940, when Yugoslavia wanted to pass anti-Jewish laws to appease the Nazis on their doorstep, Korkut wrote a paper called 'Anti-Semitism is Foreign to the Muslims of Bosnia and Herzegovina', to remind his country about their long tradition of religious coexistence."[82] Sadly, the story is barely known outside of Bosnia. The Haggadah he saved has now been placed on UNESCO's memory of the world register

The Ottomans empowered the diverse faith communities under their rule to govern themselves using their own religious laws, collect taxes as well as maintain order. This was done through the traditional Ottoman 'millet' system.

When Ottoman power began to decline from the eighteenth century, this had reverberations across all of its lands. This, coupled with the growing nationalism movement across the world, led to an increased fervour to separate from Ottoman rule. The Balkan states were aided by European powers and Russia to obtain independence from the Ottoman Empire.

According to author, Ayse Osmanoglu, the nationalist movement was spearheaded by the Europeans in a bid to destroy the Ottoman Empire which was multi-ethnic, multi-racial and multi-religious. The idea was to encourage a desire for people to govern themselves on ethnic and religious similarities, which consequently would sever hundreds of years of coexistence. Osmanoglu says, "The flames of nationalism were now being fanned in many parts of the Empire by the European Powers with a view to seizing the Ottomans' rich and strategically important lands."[83]

The nationalism movement forged new identities based on secularism. Religion, especially Islam, was not welcome. In the Balkans, as with many other lands where Muslims were in a minority, there has been an increased effort to erase the Muslim history and legacy, and create either a purely Christian or secular narrative.

According to the Folkdance Footnote's blog, "Minorities like Roma or Turkish-speakers, or Muslims were not represented–the ideal citizen was white and spoke the majority language. All were to form one seamless whole. In order to give to all equally, the state required equal participation–no 'mistresses' to divert energy and loyalty, like another language or a religion. Emphasis was on

• Bosnian dancers

the masses, not the individual. One was supposed to sacrifice one's present comforts and identities in order to build a better future for all."[84]

In Bosnia, getting rid of Muslim presence included mass killings. There was also a desire to eradicate Muslim monuments such as the famous Mostar Bridge, which was commissioned by Ottoman Sultan, Suleiman the Magnificent in the sixteenth century. Hussain says, "The targeted destruction of Mostar's Stari Most (or 'Old Bridge') was probably one of the most successful examples of the cultural genocide inflicted on Bosnia's Muslim heritage during the Bosnian war."[85] Hussain describes the bombing of mosques and monuments during the genocide. He adds, "Targeting the mosque had been deliberate. In any war, bombing monuments of heritage and culture tells your enemy you are going for their identity - by destroying the very things that make them who they were."[86]

In *Minarets in the Mountains*, Hussain further highlights all the surviving elements of Ottoman rule in Bosnia. Much has been destroyed, but surprisingly there is still a lot remaining. Along with the local populations, and support from the Turkish Cooperation and Coordination Agency (TIKA), a great deal of the destroyed elements are being rebuilt. There is also the Ottoman Muslim legacy found in mannerisms such as hospitality and looking after travellers, but also in the DNA of the people and the living legacy of Islam in the Balkans.

Sufi heritage has a strong presence in the Muslim populations of the Balkans. This is very much an Ottoman legacy too, as they were known to patronise Sufi scholars and practices. There are still some Sufi Tekkes (lodges); although they are not used to the extent that they used to be. The Bektashi Sufi order, a Shia strand of Islam, is very popular in the Balkans and most notably in Albania.

Journalist, Esma Kucukalic, says, "Sufi influence is a cohesive element of Islam in the Balkans, a living tradition and a conscious practice in accordance with rules that are inseparable from the behaviour of the dervishes. The Sufi tradition of the Balkans dates back to the 15th century, when several orders settled in the territory that would directly influence the transmission of Islam, as well as the socio-cultural, economic and architectural fabric of the region."[87]

Sadly, the Sufi brotherhoods were banned for a time in Yugoslavia, but were allowed to practice again in 1974. Since then, Sufism is regaining its popularity and traditions in the Balkans. In Bosnia, for example, the practice of Sufism has been a powerful healing practice in the aftermath of the terrible genocide inflicted on the Muslims. "In post-war Bosnian society, severely punished by the losses of loved ones and social ties, the Sufi practice still provides spaces of coexistence and the search for cures for wounds beyond the war,"[88] according to Kucukalic.

The Ottoman Muslim past, which has been targeted for destruction, is too deep-rooted to completely eradicate. One of the cultural legacies is in the music and dance of the region. The sema and dance of the whirling dervishes is commonly found in the Balkans, and it shares the Ottoman style. The music in the land is also influenced by Ottoman music traditions and likewise the folk dance heritage. However, it is very difficult to find detailed information about the Ottoman links due to cultural appropriation and attempts to obliterate the impact of Muslims. Writers Tamara Karača-Beljak and Jasmina Talam state, "One can positively say that Oriental influence was crucial in the development of instrumental music making, spiritual music and shaping of B-H urban music practice."[89]

From social occasions and celebrations such as weddings and the instruments used in countries like Bosnia, there is a clear link with the Ottoman past. Nicolae Roddy says, "Many of the region's instruments were inherited from Ottoman times, when Janissary bands used loud wind instruments like the zurna, an instrument similar to the Western oboe, but with a fuller, more cutting sound, and the boru, a type of trumpet (Locke: 116)."[90] There is also the tambura which is common in other Muslim lands across the Silk Road. According to Karača-Beljak and Talam, "Long-necked lute type, known by the common name of tambura among people. It is a fact that these instruments are of Oriental origin, although Bosnian people adjusted them to their own needs and made them in somewhat different variants (sic)."[91]

Folk dance across the Muslim Balkans shares many similarities with those across the former Ottoman Empire. Roddy says, "For example, the typical čoček, a Balkan dance especially popular among Muslim Roma and Albanians, is characterized as 'an improvised dance, utilizing hand movements, contractions of the abdomen, shoulder shakes, movement of isolated body parts such as hips and head, and small footwork patterns, ... clearly an heir to the dances of the Ottoman çengis, but its subtlety and restraint distinguish it from contemporary belly dancing (Silverman: 127).'" [92]

The cocek dance and music style is a Turkish dance that came with the Ottomans to the Balkans. It is traditionally a dance that was performed by young boys, partly due to the controversy of women performing dance in public spheres. The meaning of 'cocek' comes from the Persian word 'kuchak' to mean 'young' or 'little'. It was more often performed by non-Muslim boys and often Romanis which is why it is often now called the Gypsy dance. However, it is Ottoman in origin.

There are many other folk dances performed across the Balkans, such as kolo and horo, which are popular across all communities, and adapted to each area's own culture and norms. The Muslim lands will practice mainstream dances, but have elements incorporated from their traditional Islamic and Ottoman heritage. These practices have become part of their identity for centuries, although the root is not always obvious unless you dig deep into the history. The religious links have sadly been stripped away. Although, you can still find the stories by speaking to people, as thankfully the traditions and stories have been passed on.

• Tartar dancer

9- The Story of Tatar Muslims

Islam has over a thousand-year connection in what is now modern-day Russia. There are a large number of indigenous Muslim communities who continue to live in this huge country, including the Tatars and Chechens.

The Tatars were originally a nomadic tribe living in North-Eastern Mongolia. They spoke a Turkic language and officially embraced Islam in 922. In fact, Muslims have lived in Russia almost since the advent of Islam, even before the Tatars converted, as there were other tribes and communities who migrated there. As a result of such a long and lasting presence, Muslim culture in its various forms is embedded in the traditions of the people. Historian, Dr Stef Keris concurs that Muslims are a core part of Europe, "They keep calling this continent a Judeo-Christian culture and civilisation but we should add to it, Judeo-Christian-Muslim civilisation and culture as well."[93]

The Tatars lived predominantly in the European part of Russia, near the Volga River or what was known as the Golden Horde. They had their own state from the seventh to the thirteenth century. After 922 when they officially adopted Islam, this became a Muslim state. However, they moved deeper into Western Europe after clashes with the Mongols. Tatars spread to areas such as Poland and Lithuania, and have a historic presence in these countries as well. They also intermarried with the local population, thus spreading their culture even further.

In the late fourteenth century, the Golden Horde split into various independent Tatar Khanates of Kazan, Astrakhan on the Volga River, Sibir and Crimea. Volga Bulgaria was positioned along the Silk Road, which meant exposure to Muslim traders, faith and culture. This included the influence of different Muslim dance styles.

In 922 AD, Ibn Fadlan, a traveller and theologian, was sent by the Abbasid Caliph in Baghdad as an envoy to visit the King of the Bulgars of the Middle Volga. The Muslims called the Vikings in this area 'Rus,' and when Ibn Fadlan visited them, he made detailed accounts of their customs, dress, and religion, even witnessing a Viking ship cremation ceremony. These were recorded in what is known as his Risala (account/journal). From here, we get a great deal of useful information about the ways of the Vikings from this area.

Ibn Fadlan's work also highlights that Vikings were regularly trading with Arabs. The Arabs were historically accustomed to travel and trade, and encountering different people and their customs. In fact, many Arabs, not only Ibn Fadlan, wrote accounts of their encounters with the Vikings, and these are proving to be very useful historical documents. Archaeologists have also come across Arabic dirham coins in Viking gravesites.

We know there has been a historical Muslim presence in Russia, as well as interaction with Muslims. However, the connection of Tatars and other Muslim communities in Christian Russia has been complex, mirroring what happened with Muslim communities in other parts of the world. After the region was conquered by Russia in 1522, Muslims could not practise their religion and had to forcibly convert to Christianity. They had their culture and identity destroyed, including historical monuments and mosques. However, many continued to practise their faith secretly.

Catherine the Great reversed this policy in the eighteenth century, and again allowed Muslims to freely practise their religion. Islam continues to exist in Russia to this day, albeit with difficulties, hostility and restrictions.

The Tatar language used the Arabic script, which in 1917 was replaced by the Latin alphabet and then the Russian Cyrillic alphabet in 1939. Much of the language still has Arabic roots or words. An article in The Moscow Times echoes this, "Before the 1917 revolution, the Tatar language was written in the Arabic alphabet. In the Soviet Union, a new Latin alphabet was first introduced, then in 1939 it was replaced by Cyrillic, which is still in use today."[94]

There is now a Tataristan republic in Russia, and alongside Bashkortostan, has a majority Muslim population. The world-famous ballet dancer Rudolf Nureyev, born in 1938, was a Muslim Tatar by heritage. Both his parents, Hamet and Farida Nureyev, were Tartar Muslims. In his autobiography, Nureyev said, "My mother was born in the beautiful ancient city of Kazan. We are Muslims. Father was born in a small village near Ufa, the capital of the Republic of Bashkiria. Thus, on both sides our relatives are Tatars and Bashkirs. I cannot define exactly what it means to me to be a Tatar, and not a Russian, but I feel this difference in myself. Our Tatar blood flows somehow faster and is always ready to boil."[95]

Due to many years of Westernisation and communism, much of the Muslim heritage and practices have been watered down, forcibly eradicated or the connection lost. This has resulted in the younger generation of the Tatar community becoming more secularised and losing their Muslim identity. However, there are also some Muslim cultural practices which are so deeply embedded, that perhaps younger people are unaware that the origins lie in the faith of their forefathers. This is especially pertinent to dance traditions.

TATAR DANCE

During the period of modernisation and nationalism in Russia, the state felt it was necessary to try and create a uniform identity for the multiple communities living there. These were disparate communities, and a mix of mainly Muslims and Christians. Even within the same religion, there were different cultural practices.

Due to Russia's historical conflicts with Muslims, there was also a drive to recreate identities and history, leaving out the influence and impact of Muslims in the land. Throughout this book, I have highlighted this repeated pattern of behaviour from Western nations in dealing with Muslim citizens.

Dance in some ways has filled the gap of religion. Since the twentieth century, dance has played a massive role in nation building, and was a tool used by many new states to create one universal identity. Russia is not unique in attempting to create official state-constructed folk dances, merging several local traditions, yet without clarifying the origins and stories behind the dance, particularly of Muslim culture. Muslims were not credited for their contribution to dance because of the nature of the relationship and the desire of Russia to eliminate the Muslim element from its history.

The other difficulty with distinguishing Muslim dance culture is the treatment of dance within aspects of the orthodox Muslim community. In her PhD thesis, Diana Takutdinova writes extensively about dance in the Tatar community, and the influence of the Muslim religion on dance practice and style. She states, "It was hard for me to find an academic literature which discusses the topic of Islam in Russia in connection to dance."[96] However, despite the lack of academic work on the subject, she observed the Muslim influence through speaking with local people and studying the dance forms. "Despite the previous ideology, Islam still seems to have a significant influence on the way how to perform Tatar folk dance (sic)."[97]

The first obvious signs of the 'Muslimness' of certain folk dances is the modest clothing and 'appropriate' mixing of the sexes. Often the dances are performed separately by men and women, or the closeness is limited. Takutdinova says, "For instance, basic Tatar folk costume more or less corresponds the Islamic norms. A woman wears pants under the dress, has traditional hat or veil tight specifically in Tatar manner and has the long sleeves in the dress. Very often apron is the significant element put on top of the dress (sic)."[98]

There are two dances which stand out that contain obvious Muslim elements. There is the Altyn Basu dance where the women use handkerchiefs as veils across their face. This element is still used even in non-religious circles. "Altyn Basu dance is an intangible cultural heritage of people in the Urmai village. From Professor Laszlo's archive of 1993, in the interview by the local women it was explicitly said that their elders and they were dancing with the handkerchiefs when utmost were young (sic),"[99] states Takutdinova.

The other dance is the Recruit's dance, the story of which is to symbolise young men going to fight wars. The dance is a goodbye ritual. As they are leaving, they perform a dhikr or remembrance of God, as they do not know if or when they will return. Takutdinova states, "Recruit's dance started with dhikr represented faithfulness. Proximity between man and woman was wide enough. That position indicated that man and woman dance separately (sic)."[100] The dance also sometimes merges with the Altyn Basu dance, as the women give their floral handkerchiefs to the departing young men.

Sufi poetry is a strong part of Tatar culture, as with other Muslim cultures in Central Asia and along the Silk Road. The words of Sufi poems were put to music and incorporated into folk dance. The Moscow Time reports, "Tatar literature is best known for its poetry; the traditions date back to Sufi poetry, which was prevalent from the second half of the 16th to the end of the 19th century."[101]

10-Central Asia-The Crossroads

As the Silk Road is a core part of this dance history journey, Central Asia is the focal point. Due to its geographical position, Central Asia sits at a crossroads where many different people met, and as a result it has been a melting pot of many traditions and dance styles. The culture of this region has heavily influenced India and Pakistan, which is why it feels very familiar to me personally.

Central Asia is a massive region that now includes the former Soviet republics of Uzbekistan, Tajikistan, Kazakhstan, Kyrgyzstan and Turkmenistan. It borders with Russia, China, Iran and Afghanistan. Before borders existed, there were no man-made boundaries that stopped all these areas interacting and influencing one another.

The Central Asian region has a millennia-old history. It has seen many empires cross its path and leave their influence. Islamic empires too have had a lasting legacy, and the culture that was created under the Muslims continues to have a massive impact. In the fourteenth century, under Temur (Tamerlaine), "Samarkand became the centre of political, scientific, and cultural life."[102] According to the academic Razia Sultanova. When Temur ruled, Central Asia was considered to be at its 'golden age'. He patronised the arts, culture and dance. Sultanova adds, "Temur the Great celebrated each of his victories, diplomatic successes, and family events (especially weddings) splendidly, with music, poetry and dances."[103]

Temur has a mixed and controversial reputation. Much of the negativity stems from an underlying anti-Muslim sentiment which paints him as a one-dimensional character. Modern-day commentators, who dislike Temur, seem to be influenced by Orientalist writings and look at him through a modern lens, rather than consider the time in which he lived, where conquest and protecting one's lands from invaders was commonplace. This same comparison is not always reserved for other conquerors in history.

Being of Mongol descent, Temur was a strong and capable ruler. It was from him that the Mughal Empire in India descended. Temur was Babur's great-grandfather, and the latter was the first Mughal Emperor of India. The Mughals saw themselves as Timurid rulers, and the Central Asian legacy of the Mughal Empire was so impactful that it is still embedded in Indian culture and heritage.

Bollywood actors, Saif Ali Khan and Kareena Kapoor, named their first son Taimur in 2016, and consequently received hostile Islamophobic backlash and trolling on social media due to some perceptions of Temur the Mongol ruler. In Elizabethan England, well-known English playwright, Christopher Marlowe (1564-1593), also exploited Temur's story to create a play named 'Tamburlaine' that would feed into stereotypes of the Muslim world. The play was fictional and depicts Temur as a war-hungry barbarian. However, as much as the British public reviled him, Marlowe had created a character that the audience secretly admired and found charismatic. The story of an exotic ruler and empire was exciting for the vast majority of British people, who had little real knowledge of the Middle East and Asia.

There is another interesting side to the story of Temur, and as much as the anti-Muslim rhetoric tries to paint him purely as a villain, his legacy suggests a more nuanced character. This includes the beautiful architecture in Central Asia, and the music and dance legacy. Some of the architecture still stands to this day; magnificent blue buildings, imperial domes, Islamic calligraphy and geometric patterns.

When Muslim rule came to Central Asia in the eighth century, the land very quickly became a centre of civilisation, learning and trade. Many great Muslim thinkers and scientists, including Al-Khawarzimi, Abu Rayhan Biruni, Al-Farabi and Ibn Sina (Avicenna) came from this region; it was a hotbed of ideas and innovation. It was not in the interest of Muslim empires to destroy what was in their new lands. As minority rulers, they initially saw the need to build bridges and work with the local population for a more harmonious empire. Peter Frankopan says that the conquerors, "Were in a chronic minority, which meant that working with the local community, was not so much a choice as a necessity."[104]

It has been well-documented and evidenced that Muslim empires integrated local traditions with their own cultural and Islamic principles. Muslims valued education and learning, including from other people and lands. It is the Muslims who preserved heritage from different cultures, such as from the ancient Greeks and Persians, translating their works and building on their teachings.

This amalgamation of local traditions with the existing heritage of Muslim empires created unique and unrivalled cultures with an undercurrent of Islamic principles. Peter Frankopan says, "Cohabitation of the faiths was an important hallmark of early Islamic expansion–and an important part of its successes."[105] As a result of these principles, many ancient folk dance practices remained in Central Asia, but were fused with the cultural norms of the new rulers, creating distinctive art forms.

Across Central Asia, dance has been an integral part of everyday life and accompanied all significant events; births, weddings and holiday festivities. Professional dancer and academic, Tara Pandeya says, "Dance is an integral part of life in Central Asia; it can be seen both in rural settings and on the proscenium stage, from highly developed virtuosic classical styles to nuanced and subtle folk-dance forms."[106]

Folk dance has evolved over the years, but it can show us how societies lived and worked in the past, and in Central Asia the dance narrative really does tell a story. Pandeya adds, "Central Asian dance is highly diverse and each regional style is evocative of its environment, acting as a living link to the land."[107]

Before the creation of borders, it was common to see similar dance styles spreading across vast regions in Central Asia. One of the commonalities across dance in this region is the donning of braids by the women, who perform these dances. This can also be seen worn by dancers in the Uyghur community. Pandeya states, "Central Asia did not always have clear political, national, or cultural boundaries; it is therefore not surprising that girls with long braids are used as a visual symbol of antiquity throughout Central Asia."[108] This tradition is continued in the modern age, as folk dancers will wear their hair in this style.

In Central Asian dance styles, one can also find many examples of Muslim symbolism. This shows the seamless merging of the ancient past with Islamic heritage. In her PhD thesis, Sonia Hinz states that characteristics such as the incorporation of zarb (rhythm), charkh (spinning) and lateral symmetry in Central Asian dance come from the same source as Islamic art. "These characteristics of zarb, charkh, repetition, and lateral symmetry are not only sensually pleasing, in that they please the visual and kinaesthetic senses, but they are also common characteristics of 'Islamic' art, in a general sense."[109] Gocer validates this point by stating that, "Symmetry is based on geometrical foundation of Islamic calligraphy, which often acts as a model for other Islamic arts."[110] Therefore, the use of symmetry in some Central Asian dance has a clear link with other Islamic art principles. This is fascinating, as when you actually break down the dance moves, many are based on geometry, a form of mathematics commonly used in Islamic works of art and architecture.

The influence of Central Asian Muslim culture has extended deeply into large parts of the Muslim world. It travelled along with the descendants of rulers from this region who went on to rule large and powerful empires along the Silk Road. As a result, Central Asian dance heritage plays a huge role in other Muslim dance cultures, due to its centrality to the Muslim historical narrative.

SHAMANISM

As well as the influence of Islamic culture on dance in Central Asia, there was also considerable pre-Islamic influence. Shamanism was the ancient belief system in Central Asia. This includes the veneration of the natural and spirit worlds, and there were many rituals that involved movement and dance.

With the advent of Islam, Shamans would incorporate Islamic culture into their rituals, gradually a cultural fusion occurred. This was most likely stronger in the early days of Islam, but some Shamanic elements have been watered down over the centuries. Academic Razia Sultanova states, "Pre-Islamic religious practices have been integrated deeply with local traditional culture and art...However, the present religion, Islam, having a long association with culture and art, has produced many fundamental links with music."[111]

As with many ancient cultures, Central Asia has a massive oral tradition, and the rituals of Shamanism have been practised and passed on through generations. Some of the elements have remained, and have had an influence on the dance movements that are still present today. Sultanova says, "Central Asia did not experience an industrial revolution on the same scale as Europe. Artists inhabit, embody, and understand both worlds...For this reason, professional dance artists in Central Asia are well equipped to straddle the past and present, acting as time travellers, transporting their audiences into liminal spaces."[112]

Sultanova argues that Shaman rituals, especially among women, are still very much alive in Central Asia. Women are the guardians of this legacy. "Traditional forms of Shamanism are preserved among the Tajiks and Uzbeks... Shamans have different helping spirits, and different healing and fortune-telling practices. Instead of the drum (or sometimes additionally), a lash, a sieve, a wooden serving spoon, a staff, a mirror and a cup with water are used as ritual objects."[113] These rituals and objects would have been incorporated into the dance styles.

THE IMPACT OF SUFISM ON CENTRAL ASIAN DANCE

In addition to pre-Islamic Shamanic rituals, Sufism has had a huge influence on the cultural practices of Central Asia. This is one of the areas, including Mesopotamia and North Africa, where the main Sufi orders hailed from, and their popularity spread in this region and beyond, deep into the Islamic world.

The Sufi dhikr or sema, can include poetry, music and dance rituals. The most famous dance ritual is the dance of the Whirling Dervishes, which was founded based on teachings of Jalal ad-Din Rumi, the famous thirteenth century Muslim poet and philosopher (see Chapter 5). The sema is practiced all over Central Asia, and has influenced the various dance styles across the different regions.

It is really beautiful to observe how in Central Asia, pre-Islamic and Islamic cultures have seemed to seamlessly merge across cultural areas, including dance. I will explore the regions and prominent dance styles of Central Asia in more detail.

UZBEKISTAN

Dance in Uzbekistan is varied in its detail. But, with all its expressions, it is a beautiful depiction of a vibrant Uzbek culture. Uzbek dance has both classical and folk dance traditions.

There are three distinct Uzbek classical dance schools: Ferghana, Bukhara and Khorezm. The similarities are the movement of the upper body, graceful arms and hands, and animated facial expressions. They do not use much pelvic movement as with Middle Eastern dance. Folk dance, however, is more universal and practised across the whole region and has been passed on from generation to generation.

In this region, one of the most beautiful living legacies is the shared Jewish and Muslim musical styles called the Shashmaqam, which also has an accompanying dance form.

SHASHMAQAM: A JEWISH/MUSLIM SHARED HERITAGE

Shashmaqam is a uniquely Central Asian type of music style. The centuries-old Shashmaqam classical style originated in the ancient city of Bukhara, Uzbekistan.

Professional dancer and academic, Tara Pandeya, says, "Central Asia has ancient and classical music and dance tradition. Shashmaqam (meaning the 'sixth maqam' in Persian). This classical tradition was patronized in the multi-ethnic royal courts of Bukhara and Samarkand by the Emirs and has been around for over a thousand years."[114] It is deep-rooted in Sufi traditions and the sema. In 2008, Shashmaqam was placed on the UNESCO Intangible Heritage List.

Shashmaqam lyrics come from classic Sufi poetry written by revered Sufis in this region, including Hilali, Mashrabi, Badil, Khussroa and the Mughal princess, Zebunisa-the daughter of Emperor Aurangzeb. Zebunisa was a talented poet. She was also a Sufi, and wrote devotional poetry with traditional Sufi themes and imagery. In this way, she was said to have been influenced by her talented aunt, Jahanara Begum, who was also an accomplished poet. The princess patronised poetry and the arts and aided in the publishing of many great pieces of literature. This was all through her own personal allowance.

Her pen name was 'Makhfi', which means 'the hidden one', and her collection of poems is called Diwan-i-Makhfi. She also wrote several books. The connection between Mughal India and Central Asia is also apparent through the influence that Zebunisa's work had in this area.

Shashmaqam music is calm and sophisticated, and is played on instruments such as long-necked lutes, frame drum, which is similar to a tambourine, and the tanbour, which is like a bass fiddle.

Professor Alexander Djumaev says, "It is a refined sort of music, with lyrics derived from Sufi poems. Despite this close relation to Sufi ideas and an overall perception of the genre as a way to reach the divine, however, the history of Shashmaqam (from the Persian/Tajik for 'six modes'), is intertwined with Central Asian political history."[115]

While music and poetry are the main focus of Shashmaqam, dance supports the portrayal of the piece. The dance which accompanies the Shashmaqam music needs to be spiritual and heart-felt. You cannot dance this authentically without the connection to God. Sonia Hinz states, "Of all the dances I learned and saw in Tajikistan, Shashmaqam was the style of dance most often equated with the spirituality and antiquity of Tajik culture and, therefore, required the most expression, emotion, heart, or soul, depending on to whom one talked."[116] It is a popular dance in Central Asian culture, and reflects the deeply rooted connection to Sufism and the sema traditions. Dancers don a small purse which is said to represent the Qur'an. This dance tradition connects Central Asia to the rest of the Muslim world, where they also have dance traditions that are rooted in devotionalism.

Bukhara, under the Muslim empires, was a diverse society. The development of Shashmaqam subsequently has a great deal of influence from many classical Muslim cultures that converged here, including Arabic, Iranian, Afghani, North Indian and other Islamic lands. It also has a great deal of influence from Turkic and Jewish communities, and the indigenous traditions of the Tajik people. It is a wonderful blend of all these rich traditions.

There are two types of Shashmaqam. One is a traditional and almost Sufi-like form, studied in a structured way with a teacher who passes the technique down to a student. The teaching of Shashmaqam was carried out in the traditional Central Asian way of Ustad-Shogird (Master-Apprentice); it is a more oral form of transfer. Professor Djumaev says, "Shashmaqam was not recorded in musical notes until the 19th century in Khiva. Prior to that, the knowledge and skill was transferred from a teacher to student."[117] The twentieth-century Shashmaqam, on the other, hand is influenced by the classical style, but has become more of a national political movement to assert a Central Asian identity post-Soviet colonialism.

The introduction of the European style of learning music did not mean that the old style disappeared completely. According to Professor Djumaev, "The notation did not replace, radically change, or abolish the principle of authentic (primordial) forms of the transmission of tradition. It would be correct to say that it became an 'additional guide' for the musicians of Khorezm."[118]

The dance that accompanied more recent Shashmaqam pieces is also more formal with a set choreography. Again, this is the influence from the twentieth century. The Russians brought with them the structured dance practices, as influenced by the Western world, and the formalisation of dance.

However, since a revival of Central Asian identity post-colonialism, the community are seeing the value in some of the old tradition as a link to their ancient past and identity. "The 'ustod-shogird' system began an active revival from the end of the 1980s and especially in the 1990s. The music program of the Aga Khan Foundation, in Central Asia, has significantly contributed to its revival in recent decades via a purposeful and systematic program,"[119] states Professor Djumaev.

THE ROLE OF CENTRAL ASIAN JEWISH COMMUNITY

Central Asia, in the period before colonisation, was a mixed community with Muslims, Jews and Christians. Although under majority Muslim rule, all three religions were integrated. Shashmaqam music was played by all the religions, and they jammed together, enjoying the bonding and camaraderie that the music brought with it. When we look at the relations between these three religions, Professor Evan Rapport from the New School in New York, states that, "We cannot look at it through the political lens of current times. Things were not perfect back then, but people got along."

Both Muslims and Jews were involved in the Shashmaqam, and it is overplayed that this was mainly a Jewish role, according to Professor Rapport. The Jewish community did have certain roles in communities, perhaps more than Muslims or Christians, and they were known to be particularly skilled at music and dance. They would play at court, and perhaps take a more prominent role in music and dance, especially when the Soviets colonised Central Asia, and Muslims stepped back from playing. Professor Djumaev says, "The real flourishing of Bukharan Jews' maqam performance occurred during the Soviet period, beginning in the 1920s and continuing until their mass departure from Uzbekistan and Tajikistan."[120]

The Soviets were anti-Muslim and anti-Semitic. They did not see the value of Muslim traditions, and saw them as a threat to their power. "Maqam's opponents believed that this art belonged to a feudal and bays (rich owners) past and represented the taste and aesthetic preferences of the ruling classes, leading them to claim that it could not be used to build a new socialist culture,"[121] states Professor Djumaev

What the Soviet policies did do, however, was bring women into more public facing roles, and it is from this point that one sees the prominence of women in the practice and public performance of Shashmaqam. Women may have practiced Shashmaqam before the Soviets took power, but were not given the prominence or public recognition. Professor Rapport says, "Shashmaqam was a place where Muslims and Jews really came together. There was lots of productive exchanges and collaborations in the world of music."

In the twentieth century, most Jews left Central Asia for Israel, the USA and Europe. The Central Asian Jewish community, however, have kept up the tradition of Shashmaqam in the diaspora and are contributing to preserving it. "Both Israel and the US have become home to many fine maqam musicians, among them descendants of musical dynasties from Uzbekistan and Tajikistan, as well as maqam ensembles,"[122] according to Professor Djumaev. These collaborations with Muslims and Jews do still happen, and there is a beautiful connection over a shared heritage. Professor Rapport says, "When the Shasmaqam performers, both Jewish and Muslim, travel around the world to perform, they meet each other with a wonderful camaraderie and connection."

• A Tajik dancer

TAJIKISTAN

Tajikistan has a wide variety of traditional dance styles that are influenced by the local environment and community. The clothing and mannerisms in the dance vary too.

Tajik dances are graceful and make use of arm and head movements. The land, nature and animal connection are strong in these dance movements. The Eagle dance, for example, is very popular in this region.

EAGLE DANCE

The Eagle Dance is a traditional dance of the Tajik people, and has ancient origins. The eagle has a special place in the Tajik culture. It is also an animal that is revered in many cultures for its strength, poise and fearlessness.

Tajikistan is a mountainous area, and the landscape is the natural habitat for the eagle. The Tajik people have been brought up with this beautiful animal in their midst. Folk dances have evolved through time, based on the natural environment and day-to-day activities of working the land. The Eagle Dance is one such example where nature and dance merge.

The Eagle Dance is performed by both men and women. It's spontaneous and fun-filled. One dancer begins and then invites a partner to join in. The movements imitate the flight of the eagle, with arms spread, involving spins and jumps. The female movements are slightly more delicate but with the same choreography. The dance has been passed on from generation to generation, and is performed at celebrations such as weddings and parties.

The Tajik people and their traditions are spread in regions around Tajikistan, including Xingjiang (Western China), Afghanistan, India and Pakistan. The dance is still practised across these Tajik communities. In the region of Tashkurgan in Xingjiang, the only place in China with a majority Tajik population, this dance is hugely popular. Musical instruments accompanying the Eagle Dance are the tambourine and the eagle bone flute.

SHEPHERDESS DANCE

The Shepherdess Dance is another style which is inspired by the land and a common occupation for a people living in nature. The costume for the dance is very colourful and based on the actual clothing of a Shepherdess. It includes a veil, a traditional red, long-sleeved coat and tapered trousers.

PAMIR DANCE

The Pamir Mountains border with Afghanistan, and there are shared cultural practices including Sufi song and dance, as well as mystical instrumental music.

There is a practice of Badakhshani (an area comprising parts of Afghanistan and eastern Tajikistan) music and dance from the Pamir Mountains. Due to the location in the mountains, there is a more distinct culture here than the rest of Central Asia. They have also preserved their Pamiri language which is similar to eastern Iranian languages, and have an oral tradition of poetry, with an emphasis on classical Sufi poets such as Rumi, Hafiz, and Hilali. They are mainly Shia Ismaili Muslims and have a devotional tradition.

Badakhshani dance is heavily influenced by the land. The academic Sonia Hinz states, "Land, then is both mystical and sensual, and influences all aspects of life in Badakhshan, including dance and other artistic expressions."[123] The dance focuses on graceful movements of the arms and hands. It is also very light-footed, which reflects everyday movements of the people, who have to be careful how they walk on the uneven terrain. The arm movements mimic the flight of birds, connecting to the region's animistic, pre-Islamic past.

They also practise ritualistic dances, again connected to their ancient past. There is a deathbed dance practice and dances using objects, which are likely linked to Shamanic traditions.

Like in other Muslim cultures, there is a sword style dance "sham-sherbozi" that is performed by men, which can be quite aggressive in nature. Dances in preparation for combat, are common in the Muslim world.

There are traditional dances like the "Girl with a Jug," which is almost like a fairytale story. The girl goes to the spring and fills her jug with water. She then washes her hands and face, and wipes the water over her hair. This part is quite slow. The second part builds up tempo, as the girl is so pleased with her reflection in the water that she begins to dance. The dance incorporates expressive movement of the hands and body, and it ends with a slower tempo again.

11–Uyghur Dance–Preserving the Heritage

I have a personal connection to the history and culture of the Uyghur Muslim community of Xinjiang, Western China. My maternal grandmother's adopted sister, Banu Khala (aunt in Urdu) is of Uyghur Muslim heritage. I never even knew she was adopted until I was much older as culturally she seems very Pakistani. When I was old enough to understand, I did realise that she had distinctively Central Asian features. However, in Pakistan, there are so many different looks due to the interaction of different peoples throughout history, and the close proximity to other lands including Iran, Central Asia, Afghanistan and Russia.

When Banu Khala was nine years old, her Uyghur parents sadly died in Muscat while they were on their way back from the Hajj pilgrimage in Mecca.

Uyghur dancers

My great-grandfather, Maqbul Hussain (Khan Bahadur),[124] was a diplomat and Finance Minister for British-colonised Oman at the time, and he adopted Banu Khala thereafter. She always knew about her birthplace and heritage; she also speaks several languages.

My great aunt's birth community, the Uyghurs, are a Muslim Turkic minority and are facing large-scale human rights oppression and genocide. They have been subject to arbitrary detention, invasive surveillance, and a far-reaching attempt by the Chinese government to erase their religious and cultural identity through re-education camps.

While Chinese conflict with the Uyghur Muslim minority has existed throughout the history of the Xinjiang region, the international community has more recently been made aware of a series of mass internment camps which imprison hundreds of thousands of Muslim Chinese and Muslim foreign citizens with ethnic ties to the Uyghur population. The Uyghur people have a rich cultural heritage, and alongside the oppression and genocide of the people, their history and traditions are also being eradicated by the Chinese government while the world looks on.

One of the cultural expressions being threatened is dance. The Uyghur dance tradition is beautiful and elegant and is naturally influenced by its Central Asian and Turkic heritage and connections. The dance styles, across the region, have similarities and aspects are shared with other cultures along the Silk Road. As with other communities in Central Asia, Uyghurs have a strong Sufi connection. This influence extends to the music and dance movements that have developed over the years, with the spiritual component at the core.

Academics, Dr Rachel Harris and Yasin Mahpul state, "Contrary to the common perception of Islam in the West as hostile to music, amongst the Uyghurs many traditional musical contexts are linked to the religion, largely due to the influence of the Sufis who use music to express and promote their faith."[125]

The Uyghurs have a maqam musical style, another close link to the tradition of Central Asia. It is a set of melodies and modes; the accompanying lyrics are taken from Sufi and folk poetry, Sufi ideals and epic stories. Here it is known as the twelve maqam. The lyrics that are more commonly used in this

• Uyghur dancer

area are from the poetry of Central Asian Chagatay (Turkic) poets such as Nawayi, Shah Mäshräp, Fuzuli, Mulla Belil and Zelil.

The wonderful and inclusive nature of the maqam is that it is accessible to everyone. It was played in the courts of kings, but equally it was, and still is, played by local people. It has a calming spiritual sound which is used by all to connect with the Divine.

The traditional maqam performers use a variety of instruments made from local materials, including a variety of lutes, dutar, tanbur, rawap and satar. They also use a range of other stringed instruments and drums. In November 2005, the art of Uyghur Maqam was named a Masterpiece of the Oral and Intangible Heritage of Humanity by UNESCO.

The dancing skills of the Uyghur people are renowned in the region. There is a grace and spirituality to the moves which is influenced by the Sufi inspired lyrics and a connection to God. The dance is also connected to the land and the everyday life of the people; this is a common theme across all folk dance forms across the Silk Road.

Uyghur dance is no different, and involves moves which incorporate these everyday tasks, including carrying a bowl on one's head and picking flowers. Animal imitation feature in the movements, as nature and wildlife have been central to the existence of tribal and rural civilisations, especially in the villages.

There are many varied dance styles in Xinjiang. Sanam is one of the most popular folk dances among the Uyghur people. It is a celebration dance for occasions such as weddings and festivities such as Nowruz (New Year). Dancers' movements include characteristic neck and wrist movements, and those of the elbows, eyes and fingers. The dancers may also improvise, following the tempo of the music.

Each region has their own distinctive dance. It is interesting to see that the Uyghur community also have a male bonding dance ritual called the meshrep. This is a space for the men to come together in dance and song. Traditionally it was also a place where men were reprimanded for morally transgressive behaviours such as drinking or adultery. This is particularly fascinating as it doubles up as a social dance space and a place for men to hold each other to account, similar to a community court.

Although meshrep can sometimes be a wider gathering of men and women, it is traditionally a male ritual which centres around dance and music. Dr. Harris summarises its meaning, "Basically a meshrep is a party. But it's also much more than that… Meshrep gatherings involve food, music and dance, joking, readings and an informal community court. They are an important part of Uyghur culture because they forge lasting community bonds, they support the transmission of language and expressive culture, and they provide a forum for discussion, planning, and community action."[126]

These traditional meshreps with a very long history are being targeted by the Chinese government as part of their ethnic cleansing of the Uyghur people. "These are massive abuses of human rights which violate many international norms and laws. Under these campaigns we saw the transformation of meshrep into compulsory singing and dancing sessions for Uyghur villagers, which were intended to 'cleanse' them of the 'virus' of their faith,"[127] states Dr Harris.

The Chinese government are trying to eradicate the Muslim heritage of the Uyghur people, and create a culturally uniform society across China. As history has shown, erasing the heritage and identity of a community destroys their very essence. This is obviously a worrying state of affairs, not just for Muslim people, but all socially conscious individuals across the world. In a bid to control the meshreps, the Chinese government registered them with UNESCO's list of Intangible Cultural Heritage. That way the government can take the elements that they want out of this traditional dance gathering, mainly the religious elements, appropriating and debasing the true nature and meaning of the dance form.

12- Dance Expressions of the Middle East

The Middle East, centre of the three Abrahamic faiths, is a significant area along the Silk Road trade route. The Arabs have historically been skilled traders, including the Prophet Muhammad. They would venture far and wide to trade, and consequently expose their culture to other people and lands. Their culture and traditions spread throughout lands where they traded, especially in places around the Middle East and up to North Africa.

The dances across the Middle East and the neighbouring regions share many commonalities. The folk and traditional dances have their own local histories, but one can find a variety of the most common such as belly dance, dabke and ardah (military sword dance), across most of the Middle East. The ardah was historically performed by men before a battle to show off their weaponry and to build their courage for battle.

Sadly, Arabic dance, with all its diversity, richness and storytelling, is often hijacked by a Western orientalist narrative of eroticisation, which fits in with the perception of Muslim men as sexually deviant and perverted, and women as mysterious sexual beings. The writer Mark Hay says, "Critics of Islam often couple language of the most hardline conservatives with their own narrow readings of cherry-picked Islamic texts to make the case that Islam promotes marital rape, misogynistic violence, and pedophilia (sic)."[128] Whilst sensual dance did exist in the Muslim world, it was not traditionally for public performance in front of men and was not overtly sexual by nature. Sensual and erotic are two very different things. That is not to say that there were some practices of erotic dance in Muslim lands-the sex trade, for example, is the world's oldest known profession-but these were underground activities. The primary association of the Arab world, with this erotic image of semi-naked dancing women as the norm, has detracted from the essence of the dance, its history and practice. In parts of the Muslim world, certain people have colluded with this image for the sake of tourism and making money.

Dance historian Anthony Shay states, "Dancing in the Middle East, especially the solo improvised version, of which cabaret belly dancing is the best-known example in the West, has been subjected to relentless romanticizing. Caliphs, sultans, sheiks, slave girls, veils, harems filled with scantily clad beauties, caravans, and mosques and minarets are familiar images in moving pictures."[129] Growing up with these images in Hollywood movies and beyond has embedded a negative perception of the Arab and Muslim world, and has contributed to prejudices, stereotypes and anti-Muslim hatred.

This eroticised image and interpretation of Arabic dance in the West developed as a result of orientalists' own inhibitions and fantasies. The Victorian attitudes to suppress sexuality found an outlet in visions of an exotic land. Whilst Islam is not prudish and the subject of sex is not taboo, there are separate rules for how one behaves in a public and private arena. Mark Hay says, "In fact, Islam was so open about sex that less open neighbouring Christian cultures often attempted to smear it as the faith of choice for sex-crazed deviants."[130]

Belly dance was not traditionally a dance for the enjoyment of male strangers. It has mostly been performed by women in the company of other women, although some men do also practise belly dance. Dance is not frowned upon in Islamic societies; it only becomes provocative when the performances that are meant for female eyes only or that of one's spouse are performed in front of unknown men. Shay says, "In the Middle East, performance of the dance as a professional practice is held in strong disrepute... This disrepute stems not from prudishness, but rather from Islamic mores that dictate that women must not appear uncovered in front of males who do not stand in proper kinship relation to them."[131]

Belly dance, as a vehicle for self-expression, female health and a bonding ritual with other women, was taken out of its context by some orientalists. These Western, predominantly male travellers could not easily gain access to Muslim women who customarily would be modestly dressed and not roaming the streets, especially alone. The lack of access to Muslim women led Western imaginations to concoct a fantasy which stemmed from prudish attitudes back home, as well notions of this exotic land. These men distorted the real nature of the dance practised by Muslim women and eroticised it for their own purposes.

HISTORY OF BELLY DANCE

Belly dance is one of the oldest known dance forms in the world, and has been in existence for millennia. The original belly dance and its purpose was very different to the version that is popularised in the Western world today. Belly dance in its authentic form focuses on movements of the torso, with the graceful use of the hands, arms and head. The dance features body isolations, shimmies, undulations, spins and figure eights. It is not an erotic dance designed to please men. It was born out of a matriarchal society, and was used as a ritual to celebrate femininity and prepare the female body for childbirth, as it is a dance focused on the pelvic area. Dance historian, Daniel Otero states, "This method consisted of movements to help improve the health of the female and assist her with ease when giving birth."[132]

Islamic empires, in the Middle East, were responsible for belly dance spreading in this region and beyond, as a result of trade, conquest and travel. "What started as an Egyptian cultural dance 2,200 years before and evolved into a cultural phenomena which has literally galloped across the world. Different cultures along the Middle East have argued that the belly dance originated in their respective societies. The Arab Empire had much to do with this honor in spreading the dance (sic)"[133] according to Otero. Belly dance continues to be practised in its ritual and bonding nature across the Arab world, but in some contexts, on a global stage it has been exploited and turned into an erotic spectacle.

Belly dance developed and changed on its journey along the Silk Road, where it has influenced movement in India, and consequently flamenco in Spain, which has some of its roots within the Romani Gypsy community of North India. Otero says, "Going into Europe, possibly transported by the Arab-culture itself through the subsequent invasions of Europe during the Middle Ages or the Romani (Gypsy) people, who took it via India and introduced it to Spain. The belly dance evolved from the traditional strumming and rhythms from the Middle East to influence parts of the flamenco-dance style in the following way: how the music is played, people do a roundabout motion with their hips, perform the traditional turns and certain costume elements."[134]

Once the dance became exposed to the West in the last few centuries, its spiritual nature and connection to the inner self has somewhat been exploited by those who could only see its sexual nature. And some in the Arab-Muslim world allowed themselves to be exploited for financial and other gains. There are, however, some practitioners in the west and around the world who are trying to reconnect the dance to its original purpose.

Belly dance's popularity exploded in the United States in 1893, when Arabic dancers performed at the World's Columbian Exposition in Chicago, otherwise known as the Chicago World's Fair. The Expo was a commemoration of the 400-year anniversary of Christopher Columbus's so-called discovery of the New World. Sol Brown, an American, had seen the dancers perform in Paris, and decided to bring them to America to replicate the success. He is credited with writing a song which has since become the theme tune for belly dance, 'The Snake Charmer Song.' The song was also known as 'The Streets of Cairo'.

The controversy that the dance created was phenomenal, but that also made it more intriguing and thus popular. In the West, the dance became known as 'Danse du ventre' or 'Oriental dance'. Otero states, "When it was demonstrated in the Chicago World's Fair of 1893 (World's Columbian Exposition), it certainly caused a commotion. Those who witnessed this hypnotic dance called it mistakenly so, the 'Dance of the Orient'. The problem was that once it was exposed to Western society, it was often and in a stereotypical way portrayed as a dance to entice for sexual purposes only."[135]

Although the dance caused controversy and was targeted by censors and moralists, there were many who secretly loved it and some individuals were vocal in their support. Writer, Michelle Harper says, "The dance did have its bold defenders, including Kate Field, a prominent female journalist and lecturer. Field touted its health benefits, 'Such development and control of abdominal muscles as are exhibited by the dancing girls in Chicago-Cairo would, if possessed by American women, be the salvation of the race. Invalidism would be impossible, and children would be born healthy.'"[136]

DABKE

Dabke is one of the oldest social dances in the Arab world, and the practice flourishes across the Middle East to this day. The dabke's roots are traced back to the Levant region of the Middle East which includes Syria, Jordan, Lebanon and Palestine. It is pre-Islamic in its origins, and as with most folk dances, came about as a result of day-to-day life and village activity. When villagers were working together to build homes, they would use the foot stomping action to turn the soil into thick mud, which would then be placed on the roofs. The work was made into a communal activity which sometimes included the stomping action to poetry and song, accompanied by a reed instrument and drum.

Dabke has been passed on from generation to generation, and its usage extended to social occasions and celebrations such as weddings and is performed in a line dance formation. The movement involves stepping with the left foot and crossing over the right foot. Dabke normally has a lead dancer who sets the movements for others to follow.

As time moves forward, culture and traditions also evolve. Whilst the dabke has remained true to its core of bringing communities together in communal action, in recent years it has become a tool for political activism and protest against unjust and oppressive regimes. In Syria, Akram al-Hourani, Vice President from 1943-1963, was pro-Arab unity and realised the power of the dabke to bring people together. According to academic Shayna Silverstein,

• El Funoun Dance Troupe performing Palestinian dabke

"He emphasized the dancer's rural origins in order to harness the village dance to visions of agrarian land reform and mobilization. The dabka circle embodied pan-Arab unity and stood in for a sense of homeland shared among people from villages scattered across greater Syria."[137]

In the twenty-first century, the dabke was used by young people in Syria to protest against the Assad regime. Silverstein notes, "On Fridays across the country, demonstrations occasionally break out into what might be called radical dabka. At 10 am on December 11, 2011, men and women in Aleppo chanted and rhythmically stomped their feet 'in homage to Homs' for over half an hour."[138] She continues, "Radical dabka is also a form of play and social interaction used to make meaning out of historical events. It demonstrates how Syrians have taken back the streets, as well as the cultural symbols of their national heritage."[139]

RESISTING ARREST: HOW A PALESTINIAN DANCE TROUPE THREATEN ISRAELI OCCUPATION

El-Funoun, a long-established Palestinian dance troupe based in Ramallah, have for many years been using their traditional dabke dance and music heritage to convey a strong message of resistance to Israeli occupation. Established in 1979, El-Funoun, which means 'The Art' in Arabic, is no ordinary dance collective. Since their inception, they have primarily been on a mission to resist Israeli occupation and the eradication of their people and culture.

This has been a task filled with danger and challenges. One of their members, Ata Khattab, was imprisoned by the Israeli authorities on 2 February 2021. He was kept in prison without charge. Noora Baker, Head of Artistic Production at El-Funoun, said, "Unfortunately the arrest of Palestinians is a common occurrence. People are arrested for simply being Palestinian, and being advocates for our culture and identity. Ata has been vocal about the treatment of our people, and he works to continue our traditions, as well as being popular with the community and young people. He has committed no crime."

Dancing in Palestine could literally mean a choice between life and death. The Israeli authorities view any expression of Palestinian culture and heritage as a threat, and one that could cost you everything. Noora says, "In Palestine you are imprisoned for your ideas and your values."

El-Funoun is committed to being a diverse community that includes men and women, children, Christians and Muslims. They are made up of volunteers, and have 230 members presently. Noora states, "The dance performance deliberately involves large numbers of dancers, because it is part of the message of collective action, creativity and unity."

Their activist ethos means they push boundaries. "We are an inclusive group," says Noora, "We recreate folksongs songs and produce our own choreography based on Arab-Palestinian folklore. We adapt these to represent the Christian, Muslim and minority communities in Palestine, and we always have women at the forefront."

"Our dances have roots in Palestinian folklore, and many of these have traditionally been practiced at celebrations and weddings. The dance styles have their own stories and origins that go back to even pre-Islamic times. Dance has always been present in our community as it is a form of everyday action. In traditional societies, the movements would be inspired by working the land and the natural environment," says Noora. El-Funoun incorporates these traditional moves, but adapts them to deliver a timely message.

Music style and content heavily influences dance movements. In recent times, Palestinian songs are rooted in political resistance. Women are featured prominently in the songs and are portrayed as strong and willing to fight for their land (literally).

Noora says, "We see our movement as reviving Palestinian heritage. All culture evolves through time, and this is what we are trying to be part of with El-Funoun. We don't want to be stagnant; we value and respect our traditions, but we want to appeal to a younger audience as well as reflect our reality in the present time. In the diaspora, there is more of a need to preserve culture and freeze it in time. Whereas, we are living our culture every day, and we want it to evolve."

El-Funoun are well known in Palestine and have a big following. They are a symbol of hope for the people. Before Covid-19 struck, they would perform at venues across Palestine and would have anything from 1,000 to 3,000 audience members. However, movement across the country is extremely difficult, even without the added restrictions caused by Covid. The Israeli authorities make it very tough, but this group is not easily deterred by the Israelis nor by Covid. Practice continued as best and as safely as possible during the pandemic. El-Funoun switched to virtual dance sessions, which was not always accessible to everyone due to barriers to getting online. They also continued some limited face-to-face dance practice with smaller numbers and everyone wearing a mask.

El-Funoun have been longing to return to performing live and taking their message across Palestine and the world. Sadly, life returning to 'normal' has been an even slower process for the Palestinians. While Israel was being celebrated across the world for its fastest vaccination campaign, the Palestinian people were being actively denied vaccines by the Israeli authorities, who by international law, are responsible for vaccinating Palestinians.

I am sure that the story of how Palestinians have been treated over the pandemic will make its way into the El-Funoun dance and music repertoire at some point in the near future. As Noora says, "We use the stage to show that we exist and to preserve our history."

A DANCE-OFF WITH OCCUPATION: WOMEN, POWER AND RESISTANCE

Hawiyya Dabke is an all-female Palestinian dance group based in the UK, advocating for the preservation of Palestinian identity and culture.

In Arabic, Hawiyya means identity; a name befitting this group of women who are fighting for the survival and freedom of the Palestinian people. This dance collective is first and foremost a group of social activists, who use dance, performance and poetry to raise awareness of a brutal occupation.

Shahd Abusalama, one of the founders of the Hawiyya Dabke dance troupe says, "We use our performances to promote social justice for Palestinians and other oppressed people, and to celebrate our culture which has been suppressed for decades. Israel has long tried to appropriate the indigenous traditions and arrest, harass and restrict dabke dancers and other artists. We will not allow our culture to be appropriated and defaced by our oppressors!"

Shahd says, "Dabke is about rootedness, belonging and unity. There is a traditional dabke song 'Ala Dalouna' which means 'let's go and help', and is now used as a call for all Palestinians to join together in resistance."

From the end of the nineteenth century, Jewish settlers started arriving in Palestine. With the creation of the state of Israel in 1948, settlements increased drastically and continue to expand to this day. Many of these settlements are deemed illegal by international law. Yet, Palestinians are still being forcibly removed from their homes. The forced evictions in occupied Jerusalem neighbourhoods, Sheikh Jarrah and Silwan in May 2021 sparked widespread condemnation, and put the spotlight on a crisis that has been going on for decades, and has intensified to an unprecedented scale post October 2023.

Since 1948, a large number of Palestinians have become refugees scattered across the world, and are not allowed to return to their homeland while Jews from anywhere can claim citizenship under the Law of Return. The Palestinians who remain are basically prisoners in this land with no rights or freedom.

However, Palestinians are a resilient and creative people. Where they have been silenced, they use other means of resistance such as dance. Hawiyya run dabke workshops all over the world, and spread awareness of the Palestinian cause through grassroots projects and creativity.

Being a women-only dance troupe, it gives Hawiyya the scope to reach spaces and audiences where mixed-sex groups cannot reach, and this results in their message spreading to a wider crowd. The dabke empowers women participants to express themselves freely, especially those who have suffered from trauma or abuse. They connect to the message of the dance and can use it to release their own suffering.

Nadia Sibany is a Hawiyya collective member and dancer who grew up in Nablus and came to the UK when she was just seven years old. She joined the group in 2018 after searching for a way to connect more closely with her Palestinian heritage. Nadia has been dancing from a young age, but was not trained in dabke. However, with the worsening of the situation in Palestine over the years, and a sense of isolation from her people, she wanted to be part of the fight for justice.

• The Hawiyya Dance Company performing Palestinian dabke

She says, "I joined Hawiyya because it combined my thirst for social activism with my love of dance. I wanted to be part of a movement which serves as a cultural and political unification for hundreds of thousands of Palestinians denied the right of passage or return to their homeland. Being part of Hawiyya has given me this sense of identity and purpose."

Nadia adds, "I love the fact that this is a women's dance troupe. We are all from diverse backgrounds, and united for the Palestinian cause. Dabke is traditionally seen as a male-led dance, but we are mixing this up and bringing dabke to the present and the future. Women bring a unique perspective to this dance as mothers, sisters, aunts, wives and daughters, and we interpret the movements based on our experiences and realities."

As a UK based group from London, Hawiyya's existence brings the story of the Palestinian people to the British public, in a relatable way through arts and culture. Nadia says, "The brutal occupation, when heard in the news, can seem distant. However, when the reality is depicted through a beautiful and emotionally charged performance, the audience can imagine the horrors of living under occupation."

With the sad state of affairs in Palestine, it is easy to feel powerless. However, Shahd states, "I feel power when I dance the dabke!" She adds, "We have hope, as we don't have the luxury of despair. Palestine is a reason to live for. Recently, I have seen many more people mobilising, and there has been an increased awareness about what is happening to the Palestinians. The Israelis are losing the moral battle. We are living in a world where Palestine is being erased from the map. We want to remind the world that we exist, and that we have a beautiful history and culture. And despite Israel trying to destroy us, we will not be erased!"

ARDAH SWORD DANCE

The Ardah is a traditional sword dance that comes from Arabia. It has also been named as the national dance of Saudi Arabia, and its roots go far back in history. It is a dance that was mainly performed by men, but this has changed over the years and women often take part too.

The Ardah is a military dance that was performed before a battle. The strong, powerful movements to a loud drum beat would prepare the fighters psychologically for the battlefield. It is performed with two lines of men (or women) standing shoulder to shoulder, with an ammunition belt around them and holding a sword in the right hand. Soldiers would recite poetry and move, side stepping in synchronicity with the drum beat. The dance, with its historical roots, is now mainly used as a symbol of nationalism across the Middle East.

13- Iran—Meeting Point of History

Iran, a country which has received a copious amount of negative publicity in the West, was an advanced civilisation, and continues to have a beautiful culture and heritage with deep roots in the past. It also has a long history and tradition of dance and music.

Persia, as Iran was previously known, was a key location on the Silk Road, and has had a multitude of different peoples and empires cross its path that made this area their home, from Cyrus to Alexander the Great to the Sassanids, Seljuks, Timurids, Safavids and the Qajars, to name a few. This has resulted in a very rich and diverse culture, which is reflected in the dance culture as well.

Dance forms in Iran have been influenced by landscape, external cultures, and neighbouring regions. Persian/Iranian culture has also largely influenced culture in Muslim-ruled India. Persian was the official language of the Mughal Court until the British replaced it with English; however, there are still many

Persian words in Urdu to this day. Classical Urdu poets wrote poetry in Persian as well as Urdu; in fact, it was considered to be a higher standard of work if it was written in Persian. Author Mehr Farooqi echoes this point, "But we must not forget that Persian in India, even at the end of the nineteenth century, and in spite of the colonial emphasis on modern, Western education and vernaculars, was very much a part of the literary-cultural fabric in most of the subcontinent."[140]

As a result of Iran's geographical position and the spread of its rich culture into neighbouring regions, there are overlaps and many similarities in musical style, movement and even stories behind the dance, across Iran and other Silk Road lands.

Folk dance in Persia was influenced by ancient ritualistic elements, specifically the Zoroastrian religion. The oldest reported Persian dance is devoted to Goddess Mithra. However, as Muslims ruled Persia for well over a thousand years and created the most recent civilisation, the influence of Muslim culture has also penetrated the dance styles. As with the dance histories of all the regions I've discussed along the Silk Road, the pre-Islamic rituals were fused with Muslim civilisation and created new dance practices. However, with Islam as the dominant faith, the pre-Islamic religious elements were left out (such as worshipping multiple Gods), but the cultural elements remained.

Music has also influenced the way that dance is performed in Iran. Whereas the music in Arabic, Central Asian and Turkic cultures use the maqam style of music, Persian culture developed slightly different musical mode called dastgah. These are split into smaller units called gusheh, and are closely linked with classical Persian poetry. In Iran, the separation from the maqam style started to take place in the thirteenth to fourteenth centuries within the Timurid period. These different notes produce a uniquely Persian musical style, which in turn impacts the dance movements.

Classical Iranian poets, including Hafiz, Rudaki, Ferdowsi, Attar, Rumi, Nizami and Omar Khayyam's works, were put to music or in the absence of music, the words were recited in musical style, and dancers would use these lyrics to create beautiful dance forms. The dancers' expressions and performance would imbibe these words. Traditional Persian dance movements are very graceful and elegant, predominantly involving upper body movement with expressive looks. The dance is not sexual or sensual; it is more akin to storytelling which communicates the myths, legends and literature of the Persian people. It also has a spiritual element, especially where the poetry is inspired by mysticism.

The dance styles in Persia follow the pattern of dance found in other Muslim lands. This includes the four most common dance styles described by Lois Ibsen al-Faruqi, including solo, war and combat, chain or line and spiritual dances. Iran consists of many tribes and ethnicities such as Kurds, Armenians, Assyrians, Turks, and Arabs, so there are also a wide variety of dances from different regions, historical influences and culture.

NOWRUZ

Nowruz is the celebration of the arrival of Spring, and is also known as the Iranian or Persian New Year. The celebration is accompanied by certain rituals, food and plenty of folk dancing. It is an ancient pre-Islamic practice, and is perhaps more than several thousand years old. Although Nowruz is a religious practice for Zoroastrians, its symbolic meaning to welcome Spring and embark on a new year was not rejected by most Islamic rulers, and it has flourished in Iran ever since. Despite some efforts to suppress it post the 1979 Islamic revolution, it has survived. Not only is Nowruz celebrated in Iran, but neighbouring lands also mark the Spring festival. Some parts and communities in my motherland, Pakistan, also celebrate the Iranian New Year.

There are many ancient stories about the origins of Nowruz, but the most popular is from the eleventh century-the Iranian poet Ferdowsi's epic poem, the Shahnameh. In the poem, Ferdowsi writes about a mythical Persian King called Jamshid. The King saves the world from a winter that is set to destroy the people. He does this by building a throne which has brightly coloured gems. He instructs demons to carry him up to the heavens, and there his throne lights up the whole world. This day marked the New Year for the Persian people.

The New Year is about renewal and purification, and there are many rituals that accompany the festivities. Ferdowsi's epic is central to Persian culture and history, and many of the stories in the poem are re-enacted through

• Fahima, Founder of Shohod Arefan

dance performances that glorify Persia's past before Islamic empires ruled over the land.

IRANIAN DANCE: POPULARISED IN THE QAJAR COURT

Persian dance is very much a dance for the ordinary people, but it was also valued in the courtly setting. The Qajar Dynasty ruled Iran from 1795-1925, and under them the Persian dance forms became more formalised and flourished under the patronage of the court.

The court dances took on the form of what is now known as 'classical Persian dance' and this gave it a higher status, making it a slightly more acceptable art form in the eyes of society. It is 'classical' in the sense that the movements are learned, choreographed and passed on through generations by a teacher. However, Persian dance is not as structured as other long-standing 'classical' dance forms, such as Western ballet or Bharatnatyam in India.

Persian dance is heavily focused on the use of the upper body and arms. It is graceful and full of emotion, similar to Persian poetry and visual arts, which gives it depth and character. Pieces are inspired by the words of the great Persian poets and also scenes depicted in Persian miniatures. The poetry is often based on Sufi devotional themes, and therefore the dance has a mystical and spiritual element, as well as a connection to nature. It is distinct from Arabic dance as it does not emphasise the use of the hips. Facial expressions are a must, as without these it cannot be classed as authentic Persian dance.

Dance in Iranian culture was still seen as taboo for women to practise in front of a male audience. It faced opposition from mainstream society, which was conservative, especially after the Islamic revolution of 1979. Historian, Anthony Shay, argues against the strict condemnation of dance by patriarchal Muslim society, and feels the subject is much more complex than some scholars and writers portray. He states, "The Qur'an makes no definitive statements concerning music or dance, nor does it overtly place prohibitions on either. Islamic attitudes toward dance and music are more complex than some of these writers would have us believe."[141]

It was the strict prohibition of dance, by the Iranian society that led dance lovers to turn away from their own cultural traditions and move towards the

Western concept of dance. Iran became increasingly Westernised in the post-World War II period and ballet began to be taught by Western dancers. Many Iranians were drawn to it, as it was probably the only dance form that they could access at the time.

However, there was still a sense of pride towards Iranian dance heritage, and elements of this were brought to Western dance. Academic Nilla Cram Cook said, "When the Iranians set out to modernize their music and dance, they held their rich literature and history and the folklore of their country in the place of first importance. Bringing their own genius for beauty into play, they succeeded in creating a ballet truly Iranian and oriental."[142]

Iran became the first Muslim country to have its own national ballet company in 1958, performing all over the world. It fused classical and traditional Iranian dance styles with Western dance. However, after 1979, the dance company was closed down and dance was strictly prohibited. Dancers again went underground, and many left the country and are preserving Iran's vast dance heritage in the diaspora.

A GLIMPSE INTO THE VARIETY OF IRANIAN FOLK DANCES

BANDARI DANCE

Bandari dance is a popular folk dance from Southern Iran, and due to its location on the Persian Gulf, a strategic trade route, there are Arabic and African influences.

It is an energetic dance with a party feel that is normally performed at cultural festivals, weddings and celebrations. It can be performed in a group as well as solo, and incorporates movements of the hips, arms, hands and head. The hip movement is unusual in Iranian dance, and this is due to its proximity and subsequent influence of Middle Eastern dance styles.

Bandari means 'of the port', and as this dance practice comes from the coastal south, the dance is named after the place of origin. The dance also has a predominant feature-where dancers move their hands in a manner that is similar to movement used by fishermen at sea.

SHAMSHIR BAZI

There are many styles of sword dance in this region, particularly in the provinces of Baluchistan and Sistan. Sword dances are also common in the Middle East and North Africa and mimic a real battle. The movements include attack and defence with the pace quickening as the dance progresses.

RAGHS-E-SAMA

Sama in Persian means a happy and joyful song; it is a word that comes from Arabic. In reference to dancing, sama refers to a spiritual dance of the Sufis. As Sufism is popular in Iran, there are a great many spiritual dances that connect the dancer with the Divine. This is a very common dance form in Iran across the different regions, as well as across the Muslim world.

RAGHS-E-BALUCHI

Baluchistan is a region which is connected to Iran, Afghanistan and Pakistan. It has a distinct culture and heritage, and the dance practices are also identifiable. The main theme in Baluchi dance is the clapping of the hands. This feature is often used across the different dance styles.

RAGHSE QASHGHAYI

Qashghayies are Turkic tribes in Iran. They also have their own style of dance including a dance with shawls and bright coloured skirts for women, who also hold bright scarves in their hands. When women are dancing, they form a circle and jump while their skirts move together creating beautiful, synchronised movements.

14- Afghanistan— A Deep Rooted Culture

The recent history of Afghanistan has been a tumultuous one. Sadly, this rich, beautiful land is now associated with the Taliban, an ultra-conservative 'Muslim' group. At the time of writing, the Taliban took control of the country from the Afghan government in a shocking and sudden coup.

The Taliban are notorious for their stringent regime which stems from an austere, and many would argue, 'false' interpretation of Islam. However, this land has not always been one of religious intolerance; it is in fact a melting pot of cultures and identities. Historian, Arezou Azad, states, "Much as in other parts of the caliphate, early Islam developed in a syncretic environment in the lands that we now call Afghanistan. But unlike anywhere else in the caliphate,

AFGHANISTAN'S
CAL DANCES FESTIV
شنواره رقص های محلی
شنبه، ۴ دلو ۱۳۹۷

in Afghanistan, Buddhism fused with Zoroastrianism, early Abrahamic traditions, and local cult practices, as well as with Islam."[143]

Afghanistan sits between Asia and Europe, and in a prime location along the Silk Road. It borders Central Asia, present-day Pakistan, Iran and is not too far from China and Russia. It is a mountainous and rugged region. The harsh landscape has made it difficult for empires to conquer and control it in its entirety.

Historical figures, such as Darius I of Babylonia (500BC) and Alexander the Great of Macedonia (329 BC), conquered the land and left their imprint. The Muslim Umayyad rulers of Arab heritage initially brought Islam to Afghanistan from the seventh to eighth centuries. The first Muslim empire here was created by Mahmud of Ghazna in the eleventh century, who is still considered to be one of its greatest rulers. He was of Turkic heritage, and after his death the empire extended from Iran, through Afghanistan, to India.

The Mongols, under the leadership of Genghis Khan, also took over some of the territory in the thirteenth century. Buddhist and Zoroastrian beliefs had a stronghold in Afghanistan, and there are still historical monuments that can be found here. Some were infamously destroyed by the Taliban in 1996 when they first seized power, including the world's tallest standing Buddhas. This destruction of heritage sent shockwaves across the world.

Islam in Afghanistan firmly took root from the tenth century; however, historians have argued that this was not through forced conversion, but a gradual process of which migration played a big part. Historian, Nile Green states, "André Wink has recently argued that large Muslim populations began to emerge only with the pastoral nomadic migrations that followed the Turkic and Mongol conquests of the twelfth and the thirteenth century. His argument is effectively one of Muslim migration and resettlement rather than of conversion and acculturation."[144]

Timurid rule, with its Central Asian heritage, extended to Afghanistan, bringing the culture with it. It also brought the practice of Sufism. "The Timurids were far from the first rulers of Herat to patronize Sufis...However, because of the sheer wealth of the Timurids and the fact that their polity also encompassed large parts of Central Asia, their rule over Herat saw the arrival of the Central Asian Naqshbandi order into what is today Western

Afghanistan,"[145] says Green. This Central Asian heritage is the common thread that connects the lands across this area of the world, due to the spread of the Turkic tribes and their establishment of long-standing empires.

The Lodi Dynasty, who were part of the Delhi Sultanate of India, ruled from 1451-1526 and were of Afghan origin. Green states, "Around the same time that the Timurids were ruling over what is now Western Afghanistan, northern India was being ruled by a dynasty that can truly be called Afghan in that its rulers belonged to the Lodi tribe of Pashtuns."[146] The dynasty was ousted by the first Mughal Emperor, Babur. He was of Central Asian heritage and born in Andijan, modern-day Uzbekistan. Babur also ruled Kabul, which he used as a base for his conquest of India. The ruling dynasties from Central Asia around this time were closely tied. They were connected either through marriage, blood or by their Turkic tribal links, and their culture was dominant.

Sufism was extremely popular in this Central Asian region and Sufi scholars were patronised by the Timurids. Some historians state that this patronage was due to religious fervour, but others argue it was a political move. Academic Nushin Arbabzadah states, "Once again, there was political acumen in this choice of patronage, for the ruling dynasty needed not only Sufis and their increasingly popular fellowships on their side, it also needed the legal experts in religious law who might staff the Timurid bureaucracy or at least not declare the Timurids' policies or cultural practices contrary to the Shari'a."[147] The power and influence of the Sufi scholars grew, which is why Sufism has impacted a large part of the Muslim world around the Silk Road. From the fifteenth and sixteenth century, "Sufi Islam in Afghanistan proper became inseparable from the Sufism of Mughal and post-Mughal India, particularly with regard to the circulation of the Naqshbandi order into and out of the subcontinent,"[148] states Green.

VARIETIES OF AFGHAN DANCE

In the diverse land of Afghanistan, there is naturally a wide variety of dances that reflect the different tribes and ethnicities that live here. There are three main ethnic groups: the Pashtuns in the South, the Tajiks from the Central Asian regions in the North and the Turkic people in the Northwest. The dances in Afghanistan are inevitably influenced by all of these, as well as by Indian, Pakistani and Iranian dance forms.

ATTAN DANCE

The Attan is considered to be the national dance of Afghanistan. It has a variety of forms depending on where it is practised in the country. It is an ancient dance originating from the Pashtun tribes. Ehsan Bayat, in his blog, says, "Some experts identify the dance as an ancient pagan ceremony dating back to as long ago as 2000 BCE. At this time, the dance had no particular organized form; rather, it was simply made up of random steps and movements performed to the fast beating of drums."[149] Traditionally it has been a dance for men in the public arena, with women performing it in private. However, it is increasingly being performed in mixed-sex settings. The basic movements are in the form of a chain with up to 10 people or even more; there is no limit on the maximum number. Most often, the dhol drum[150] accompanies the dance, which begins slowly and speeds up as the dance goes on. It is rhythmic and can be very energetic.

KHATTAK ATTAN

The Khattak Attan is a military inspired dance which was influenced by the Mughal rulers of India for the battlefield. The soldiers would prepare themselves to fight and be closer to God. It is now more performance-based and involves a great deal of physical prowess, with the dancers holding several swords at a time.

LOGHARI DANCE

Loghari dance is performed by both men and women, and it uses spins and twists with abrupt dramatic stops in line with the rhythm. Men will sometimes wear their traditional turbans which are taken off towards the end of the dance.

HERATI SOLO–GHAMZEGI OR QANDEGI

The Herati Solo is a women's improvisational dance. It is a coy and feminine dance which incorporates traditional aspects of a woman's everyday life including picking flowers, combing the hair and sewing.

FEMALE WHIRLING DERVISH RECLAIMING SUFI HERITAGE

Royal Timurid women patronised Sufi institutions in Afghanistan. Nushin Arbabzadah states, "Timurid women of the ruling class played an equally significant role in solidifying the social and institutional power of Sufi Islam in medieval Afghanistan."[151] This is a far cry from the regime enforced by the Taliban in present-day Afghanistan. In many ways the Taliban regime is alien to these lands that have known women to play a prominent role in public life. "Women are represented as powerful and active agents, participating in the cultural and political life of the Timurid society, whether as political agents like Gawhar Shad or as enthusiastic patrons of music and poetry like the Mughal empress Ruqiyya Bigum (1542-1626),"[152] according to Arbabzadah.

Fahima Mirzaie, a 24-year old student, is reclaiming this heritage. She founded a Kabul-based Sufi dance and performing arts group, which has strong female leads as well as members who are both male and female. This was before the recent Taliban coup in 2021, after which Fahima was forced to flee the country.

The group set up by Fahima, called 'Shohod Arefan', which means 'The Intuition of Mystics', is continuing in exile. Fahima teaches the group the technique of the Sufi dance ritual. Some of her students are as young as six years old.

The concept of a female Sufi dance group may sound strange to a Western audience, but the connection between women and Sufi mysticism has a long history in Afghanistan and the Muslim world in general. As mentioned earlier, the first known female Sufi was a woman called Rabi'ah al-Adawiyah who lived in the eighth century, and was born in Basra, Iraq. There were many similar women throughout history.

Fahima teaches the sema (ceremony in remembrance of God through music and dance) and the whirling dervish ritual, which takes time and

patience to master. The tradition of the whirling dervish ceremony is said to have originated from the poet, Jalaluddin Rumi, whose son founded the 'Mevlevi' Sufi Order. Rumi, as well as other Mevlevi leaders, had female disciples. Women were part of Sufi spiritual ceremonies, where sometimes men and women performed side by side.

The ultra-orthodox and literal interpretation of religion in Afghanistan is a more recent phenomenon. The Taliban suppressed the practice of Sufism when they first came to power in 1996. It was starting to make a comeback, but since the 2021 coup it will most likely diminish again.

Sufism has a long-standing tradition in Afghanistan. As well as the Mevlevi Order, the Naqshbandi, Qadriyya and Chishti Orders feature prominently in the country's history. Afghanistan has been home to many Sufi saints and shrines. Devotional songs and dance were commonplace here, and their revival has given the Afghan people a route of emotional release, and a way to unburden their souls.

Afghanistan is known for its strong women, like Fahima who is certainly doing her part in connecting people to their forgotten past. Much of this work will now have to be done in the diaspora. Fahima says, "I became interested in the sema from when I was 12 years old. I tried to learn more as it fascinated me. I was one of the first female performing dervishes in Afghanistan in modern times." This was a risky move for Fahima while living in Afghanistan, as there was still instability in the country, but she was committed to her passion.

The Sufi practices had clearly not died out in the hearts of the people. The revival gained huge popularity. Fahima says, "It is a way for people to connect with spirituality and find inner peace in a war-torn country." Shohod Arefan were rehearsing in school halls in the neighbourhood, and put on performances for religious and cultural celebrations such as the birthday of Rumi. They used live music played on traditional instruments, which helped create that perfect spiritual environment and connection. Sufis believe that nature is music, and the sounds they use in their spiritual remembrance resemble these natural, soothing sounds, which are designed to penetrate the heart. There was widespread devastation when the Taliban seized power in 2021, and many artists, musicians and even Sufis had to flee for their own safety.

Fahima's story, despite having a sad twist, does remind us that women in traditional Muslim societies played significant roles, although not always gaining the recognition they deserve. Women have been key to passing on tradition, often through teaching their children or other women. Sufi tradition is also passed on in a similar way, from teacher to student. It is befitting that a woman is taking the lead in reclaiming the country's Sufi past, even if she has to do this in a foreign land for the time being.

15- The Interconnected History of India and Pakistan

Dance in Indo-Pakistani culture is a huge phenomenon, especially because of the popularity of Bollywood films. The choreography in these movies is copied for wedding dances, parties and now social media trends. When I was growing up, I would equate Pakistani cultural dance to Bollywood films, as did many of my Pakistani friends. We did not realise that there was a bigger history and variety of dance styles all across India and Pakistan.

When trying to understand and unravel the dance practices in South Asia, it is necessary to understand its very complex history. The history of this region helps us understand the people from the subcontinent, and the influences, development and practice of dance.

HISTORY OF ISLAM IN INDIA

Muslims are the second largest religious group in India. They are a very sizable minority; there are more Muslims in India than in Pakistan! The current right-wing Indian government, under the leadership of Narendra Modi, is trying very hard to erase the extensive Muslim contribution and presence in India. This is similar to what has been happening in Xinjiang, China, with the Uyghurs.

Muslim empires have ruled central parts of India since the thirteenth century. The Delhi Sultanate was the first ruling dynasty and Muslim rule continued until the end of the Mughal Empire in the nineteenth century. The Muslim rulers of India had very capable and strong women within their ranks. Razia Sultan, the first female Sultan of India, ruled the court of Delhi from 1236 to 1240. She did not want to be called Sultana, and insisted on the male term, Sultan. She was a ruler of the Delhi Sultanate, which was part of the Mamluk slave dynasty. Her father was Sultan Shams-udin Iltutmish, and Razia was his only daughter.

Iltutmish ensured Razia was well educated and trained in archery, martial arts and administration. Razia's father felt she would be a much better ruler than any of his sons. In a surprise move, he appointed her as his heir. As ruler, she would appear in public dressed in traditional male attire. She rode on elephants through the streets of Delhi, making public appearances like the earlier Sultans. She ruled efficiently, establishing law and order in Delhi. Her most trusted ally was an Ethiopian slave, Malik Yaqut, whom she appointed to a prominent position at court.

Muslim presence and influence in India actually started before the Delhi Sultanate. Muslims had been in India as early as the seventh century, when the Arabs first arrived as traders in Gujarat and surrounding areas. Arab military commander Muhammad Bin Qasim captured Sindh in 712, marking the beginning of Islamic rule in the subcontinent.

The Siddi African Muslim community are one of the oldest Muslim populations in the subcontinent, having come to India with the early Arabs. Some came as merchants and others as slaves. Many rose to high ranks in society; they were prime ministers, military commanders and senior administrators in the court. There is still a large Siddi community in India who now live along the coast of Gujarat, Karnataka, Maharashtra and Andhra Pradesh where, under current circumstances, they sadly suffer a lot of prejudice and racism. There is also a Siddi population in Pakistan.

The history of Muslims in India is long and varied. The last Muslim empire of India, the Mughals, combined all these previous Muslims influences, along with local traditions and their own heritage, and created something extra special in India. They left a lasting impact, especially in terms of architecture. The Mughals had Central Asian, Turkic and Persian cultural heritage, and saw themselves primarily as Timurids, being descended directly from Timur, the founder of the Timurid Empire. Babur (the first Mughal Emperor) was the great grandson of Timur. Indian culture has been hugely influenced by this Timurid legacy, including dance.

The Mughals ruled a Hindu majority, and tolerance and diplomacy was key to their successful rule for over 500 years. The Mughals were shrewd, and realised the benefits of working closely with the diverse populations. They made alliances and were generally tolerant of different faiths and religious practices. They created ties by marriage; the Emperor Akbar married a Rajput princess, and his sons followed suit by marrying women from various faiths and backgrounds. The Mughal court was very cosmopolitan and included both Hindu and Muslim administrators. This collaboration worked really well for a long time. There are mixed views from historians on the personalities of some of the Mughal rulers and how tolerant they were. The biggest controversy is over Emperor Aurangzeb; however, historian Audrey Truschke's recent works have dispelled a lot of the negativity towards Aurangzeb as propaganda and anti-Muslim sentiment.

India's Muslim past is a core part of India. There is a massive legacy, not least that India has a huge Muslim population to this day. The Muslim past is alive now, and not just in the DNA of its people; it is in the food, language, literature, art and architecture. The Mughals also influenced traditional Indian dance, and kathak is a combination of classical Indian dance with Persian and Central Asian influences. This will be explored in more detail.

BRITISH RAJ

The British presence in India began as a result of trade and commerce. They came as small-scale traders from the East India Company but ended up as colonisers and de facto rulers of this vast subcontinent.

Europeans had been trading in India since the fifteenth century. However, after years of rivalry between each other, it was the British who succeeded in dominating India, beating the competition from their Western counterparts. Historian William Dalrymple says, "In many ways the East India Company was a model of commercial efficiency, one hundred years into its history, it had only thirty-five permanent employees in its head office. Nevertheless, that skeleton staff executed a corporate coup unparalleled in history: the military conquest, subjugation and plunder of vast tracts of southern Asia."[153]

When King James I, of Britain, sent a royal envoy to Mughal Emperor Jahangir in 1615, the Mughal ruler was unimpressed with this visitor and the small island thousands of miles away. On the other hand, the King's envoy, Sir Thomas Roe, was in awe of the wealth and grandeur of the Mughals. Roe was trying to secure a trade deal with the Emperor, but he was not interested and saw the British as "very low priority."[154] After no success with the Mughals, the East India Company started trading in the south of India with the Deccan Sultanate, rivals to the Mughals.

Over a hundred years later, the position of the Company was to change dramatically. Many historians and writers, including William Dalrymple, state that it was the death of Emperor Aurangzeb, in 1707, that changed the fortunes of the Company, after which it was able to make substantial headway in India. The Mughal Emperors after Aurangzeb became disjointed, decadent and lacked the leadership of their forefathers and consequently the Empire's power became weaker and weaker.

There were many complexities of politics and power in India, a huge land of many different rulers and structures. The Mughal Empire (before its abolition) was the overall ruling power, but it always struggled with pockets of resistance. Aurangzeb had expanded the Empire significantly until it covered most of India, but after his death it began to unravel. Historian Audrey Truschke states, "Aurangzeb ruled for forty-nine years over a population of 150 million people. He expanded the Mughal Empire to its greatest extent, subsuming most of the Indian subcontinent under a single imperial power for the first time in human history."[155]

The decline of the Empire after Aurangzeb and the rise of local rulers and challenges to Mughal power, created the perfect setting for the East India Company to make inroads. The Company was very skilful at taking advantage of such chances when they presented themselves. With a weakening central power base, other rulers in India began flexing their muscles too and establishing rival power structures and independent areas of rule. Everyone wanted to secure a slice of power. This created instability in the country for many years.

Various Indian rulers made alliances with the British where it suited their interests and vice versa, and this allowed the Company's power to grow further. With their skill in administration and finance, and superior methods of warfare, the Company was beginning to grow into a serious force to be reckoned with.

One of the most prominent Indian leaders that refused to make alliances with the British was Tipu Sultan, the ruler of the kingdom of Mysore in South India (1751-1799). He was a powerful and wealthy Muslim ruler. Historian Kate Brittlebank describes Tipu as, "The last bulwark against British imperial desires."[156] He was referred to by the British as the 'Tiger of Mysore'. Both Tipu and his father Haider Ali were wise to the threat that the East India Company posed to India and its people. They foresaw the disaster that the British would bring to the subcontinent; however, both were isolated voices among Indian rulers of the time, who were entering into alliances with the British to suit their own needs. After thirty years and four Anglo-Mysore wars, the British managed to eventually defeat Tipu, and he was killed on the battlefield. After Tipu fell, the next big rebellion against the British was not until the first Indian war of Independence in 1857.

Cunning and manipulation tactics, along with advanced warfare, helped the British to rise to power. The Company made alliances where it was beneficial to their ambitions. William Dalrymple believes it was the British alliance with Indian bankers which really helped finance and propel their interests in India. The bankers were not aligned to any regime, and saw economic opportunity

• Pakistan-based Kathak dancer and choreographer, Nighat Chaudhry

wherever it presented itself. In this case, they saw their fortune resting with the British. In essence, the British were using India's own money to help them subjugate the country.

Although the Mughal Empire was steadily declining in the eighteenth century, the British recognised that the Mughals did hold a certain legitimacy with the local people. This was the reason they kept the Mughals as figureheads, but took the real power and fortune for themselves. The British plundered and pillaged the country for their own gain. They controlled trade and did not pay tax. The profit was all going back to London. The Indians were suffering immensely and the devastating scene for the Great Bengal famine was set.

The British acted inhumanely during the famine of Bengal in 1769 to 1770. They continued to make money from the suffering of the people, which has left a very bitter taste to this day. News of the East India Company's treatment of the Indian population was getting back to London, and politicians began holding the Company to account. Many felt that the Crown needed more control over the affairs in India, as the power and money was mainly going to this small group of rich traders. Parliament succeeded in obtaining a greater stake in the Company. They appointed a Governor-General for India, but the Company was still semi-autonomous.

This system of governance continued until the Indian uprising in 1857, which was a very serious challenge to the power of the East India Company. Indians of all faiths rose up against the British and tried to reinstate the Mughal Emperor, Bahadur Shah Zafar II. If the British had been defeated then the course of history would have changed forever. Many British men lost their lives in a desperate bid to cling to power. The uprising was a turning point for India as it resulted in the abolition of the Mughal Empire, and the Crown subsequently stepped in and took over official control of India from the East India Company. This period came to be known as the British Raj. The Raj ruled the Indian subcontinent from 1858 until Independence in 1947.

Following the Indian uprising, which was a big threat to British rule in India, the British really stamped down on the Muslim population. They firstly blamed them for spearheading the 'rebellion', which some historians state was not the case, but also because the Muslims were perceived as a threat due to their long-standing rule in India. Muslims were targeted more heavily after 1857; their institutions were dismantled, Hindus were favoured for jobs and Muslims effectively became ghettoised over time. The aftermath of the uprising left behind a traumatised and impoverished community. Muslim literature and poetry from that time reflects the decline in position and treatment vetted out by the British.

As well as British rule impacting the governance and laws of India, the cultural landscape was also affected, such as the practice of dance. The Victorians frowned upon Indian dance styles and found them too provocative. According to the Tutor Hunt website, "The advent of British rule brought a decline to all forms of classical dance as they were considered overtly seductive and unwholesome. A bill was passed against temple dancing and cultural oppression took place."[157] The British did not appreciate the different cultural dances and were not interested in them as an art form, either. Indian dancers were labelled as 'nautch' girls which was a derogatory term for women who practised such dances. As a result, Indian dance was said to have declined under British rule.

PARTITION OF INDIA

The British Raj ruled India from 1858 until Independence was gained in 1947, and a Hindu majority India and a Muslim Pakistan were created as two separate nations. The two nations are relatively young when compared to the long history of India and thus share a great deal of history, culture and heritage; however, in many ways they are also quite different.

As Muslims had been present in India for over a thousand years and ruled large parts of India for at least seven hundred years, the Central Asian, Turkic and Persian Muslim culture was dominant, especially in North India. This legacy is infused in the land, even to this day.

Muslims had been in the minority, but as they held the wealth and power, their culture had a strong presence. Historian, Shashi Tharoor,[158] blames the British for fostering their classic divide-and-rule tactic, 'divide et impera', and for creating tensions between Hindus and Muslims, which Tharoor believes ultimately led to the division of India and the creation of Pakistan.

Hindus and Muslims struggled for freedom from British rule, and this political action increased in the early twentieth century. The main proponents for the fight for Independence were Mahatma Gandhi and Jawaharlal Nehru who were Hindus and part of the Indian National Congress, and Muhammad Ali Jinnah, a Muslim, who led the Muslim League.

Nehru was President of the Congress, from 1929, and then became the first Prime Minister of India from 1947 until 1964. He was charming and well-liked by the British, particularly the last Indian Viceroy, Lord Louis Mountbatten and his wife, Edwina. Although Nehru famously donned Indian traditional attire in later years, he was an Anglophile at heart. He came from a wealthy Westernised family. As a child he was educated at the prestigious Harrow School and was consequently well versed in British ways and part of the Englishman's club. Ironically, the British would still never see Indians as equals, no matter how Westernised they were. It is also commonly believed that Nehru had an affair with Mountbatten's wife and was able to steer the discussions for the future of India in the Congress' favour. Sean Phillips, DPhil History at Oxford, said, "Caricatures do, however, still loom large in the literature, with accounts that present Nehru as a handsome, warm personality close to the 'Hollywood version of a British prince', the Last Viceroy, Lord Mountbatten, standing in opposition to that of Mohammad Ali Jinnah, who is often defined as a cold, calculating presence."[159] He adds, "Jinnah is perhaps Partition's most contested and misunderstood character."[160]

Jinnah, by leading the Muslim League and Indian Muslims, was taking up a difficult position. Indian nationalists were completely against a separate Muslim nation, and the British were no lovers of the Muslims who they saw as the instigators of the 1857 uprising. Then there was the age-old threat that Muslims posed to the Christian West, and those ingrained anti-Muslim, Islamophobic views were also at play.

Indian Muslims were very fearful of being left behind in a Hindu-dominated India, especially with rising communal tensions, and these fears were not fully appreciated or understood by the leaders of the Indian nationalist movement. Historian, Ayesha Jalal said, "The idioms deployed were Hindu idioms - whether it was Vande Mataram or the Wardha Scheme of Education. The failure of that nationalism is not adequately acknowledged. People keep talking about

Pakistan and its exclusionary nationalism but what came first - communalism or nationalism? The sense of exclusion was created by the dominant idioms that the Congress employed, despite its rhetoric of inclusionary nationalism."[161]

The situation in India now, with the rise of right-wing Hindu nationalists, gives an insight into Muslim fears pre-independence in 1947. While many Muslims wanted the right to self-governance, not all wanted a complete split with India. The vision of Pakistan as posed by Muhammad Iqbal, Indian poet and philosopher in 1930, was a federation of Muslim majority states including, Punjab, North West Frontier Province, Sindh and Baluchistan. Jinnah too wanted a different version of Pakistan as to what materialised; however, the British drew up the new borders in only 36 days, and in such a way to ensure ongoing tensions and mistrust between the two nations. Jinnah called it a "truncated and moth-eaten Pakistan."[162] However, it became a choice between that or nothing.

Partition has impacted the subcontinent significantly, and has left a dark cloud over this part of the world that remains to this day. It was one of the worst refugee crises the world has known to date; 15 million people were displaced and over 1 million were killed. The aftermath of Partition has also created a host of additional issues, including serious ongoing rivalry and tensions between India, Pakistan and Bangladesh. It is difficult to even visit family living across these man-made borders which did not exist before 1947. Also, in a bid to distance themselves from each other, Pakistan and India have tried to reinvent their culture and history, with India leaning more towards its ancient Hindu past and Pakistan trying to break with the Indian heritage that was once part of its history.

Dance has suffered a blow from the political hostilities, especially in Pakistan. Whereas dance has flourished in India post-Partition, in Pakistan it has not received the same care and attention. There are many reasons for this, including the attitudes of orthodox Muslims towards dance, but also because of the desire to sever all ties with India, including any shared cultural practices. This is a shame in my view, as this means Pakistan is cutting off a large part of its identity and leaving India to solely benefit from such a rich heritage that has been significantly influenced and shaped by Muslims.

NANI AND PAPA'S STORY

Even after 75 years, the impact of the Partition is still very much alive, affecting so many lives in India, Pakistan, Bangladesh as well as in the diaspora. My family, along with countless others, have been directly impacted. The events leading up to and including Partition, have changed the course of our history, and traumatised generations of South Asian people, including those who did not even live through Partition.

Farida Maqbul, my maternal grandmother, or Nani as we affectionately called her, had a mixture of Central Asian and Afghan ancestry, like many Indians with Muslim heritage. Her family moved and settled in Muradabad, North India, and lived there for many years. This became their home. Nani's father, Khan Bahadur[163] Maqbul Hussain was a diplomat, finance minister and close advisor to Sultan Said bin Taimur, ruler of Oman. The family lived in Muscat during the years of Partition due to his job; however, after Partition they moved to Karachi, and were lucky to avoid the turmoil because they were not in India at the time.

Conversely, my maternal grandfather, Manzoor Hussain Khan, or Papa's family were in the centre of the devastation in Delhi, and fled to Karachi in the newly created Pakistan. Papa was shot by a Hindu mob due to his religion, but he was lucky to have survived and managed to escape the communal violence in India and make his way to Pakistan alone. When he reached Pakistan, his father, Dadajan, ordered Papa to return to India to collect his mother and sisters who were left behind. Dadajan was not in Pakistan at the time because he was travelling between London and India for business.

Dadajan had some contacts in the United Nations and was able to get plane tickets and the family left via air. If they had travelled on the trains, they probably would not have made it out alive. There were many people who tragically died in this way, trying to make the journey to safety.

As refugees in Pakistan, Papa's family had very little because they had left everything behind in their home-towns and were forced to start their lives from scratch. Papa's family lived in refugee camps for a while until alternative accommodation was found. They had to share small and cramped flats with

• Kathak pose

several other families, living in poor areas of town. This was a horrendously difficult situation, but one endured by many Indians and Pakistanis.

In the 1950s and 1960s, the British began inviting people from their ex-colonies to come to Britain and help rebuild the country after the Second World War. Dadajan was already familiar with London as he would travel regularly by car for his business. In 1950, he was staying in a place in Old Street, East London, with the aim to bring his family over once he was settled. In 1962, Dadajan collected everyone in a Bedford van, and they drove from Pakistan to London via Iran, Turkey and Europe. My mum was quite young but recalls the trip with fond memories as it was quite the adventure. My family were forced to uproot again; I cannot even imagine how difficult that must have been.

My Nani was the youngest daughter of seven children. She was cheeky, charming and fun-loving. Nani spent a carefree childhood in Oman because of her father's diplomatic job, and always recalled the beautiful weather, sea and the many adventures that she went on with her siblings. She often said that those were the best years of her life.

My grandparents had a love marriage in a culture largely dominated by arranged marriages, so this was quite unique. Papa first saw Nani when she was roller skating near Clifton beach in Karachi. This was a rare sight for a young woman in Pakistan in those days, but this sums up Nani's personality perfectly. Her family were educated, cultured and the women were strong and independent. Nani's mother and elder sister smoked cigarettes until they were in their 90s. They had spent time in Iran and the Middle East where women smoked shisha. I remember Nani's elder sister smoking when I was young and never thought of it as strange or out of place in our Pakistani household.

In 1962, Nani left everything she knew and loved in Karachi and came to London with Papa and three children under seven years of age. She was only 26 years old at the time. She had to quickly adapt to a completely new country and culture, which was often hostile, racist and Islamophobic. Having been pampered in her childhood and much loved, Nani now had to find a job to help support her family. She had never worked before in her life but she didn't hesitate, especially if she needed to do this to help take care of her children. Nani was very family-conscious, and I definitely think my personality is similar to hers in this respect. Nani continuously sacrificed her own wants and needs for her children and then grandchildren. This is a very common trait in mothers and grandmothers from an Indo-Pakistani background, in my own observation.

Nani worked for many years as the Household Manager for the Nigerian High Commissioner in Belgravia, London. Mum, Khalajan and Mamojan (maternal aunt and uncle) were lucky enough to spend their childhood living right next to Buckingham Palace in the Nigerian Embassy house. Mum even went to a grammar school not far away in Chelsea. Working for the Nigerian High Commissioner, Nani met many well-known people, including Malcolm X.

When she was in her mid-forties, Nani was widowed when my grandfather Papa passed away suddenly of a heart attack while on a visit to Pakistan. This was a very young age to lose her husband; however, Nani never remarried. She played a big role in helping to raise her grandchildren. I only had one living grandparent after the age of two, and Nani fulfilled the role of all the other three without a shadow of a doubt.

Nani was a patriot, and she instilled a love of Pakistan in me, but she equally loved the diversity of Muslim cultures. She was fully supportive when my aunt married Fuad Uncle who was of Yemeni, Indonesian and Kenyan heritage, and he was welcomed with open arms into our family. He had a very close bond with Nani. They both shared a love of cooking, and would cause destruction in the kitchen when making Sunday lunch for the whole family.

Nani sadly died too soon at the age of 69 in 2005. Her legacy amongst many other things, is a diverse, multicultural family who have a love for Muslim heritage and culture. She has been one of my inspirations for writing this book. Nani was very connected with the ethos of Pakistan and its raison d'etre as a safe homeland for India's Muslims. For Nani's generation, who left the motherland for a new life abroad, Pakistan represented a deep sense of belonging. She would listen to old Hindi film songs and cry, remembering her home and all that she left behind. The songs and film culture in India, from Nani's time, was heavily influenced by Muslim culture so she could relate to the words and the context.

One of the things she really loved were the songs and dances from old Bollywood films. For Nani, the words, movements, clothing, and scenery were all reminders of her Indian Muslim heritage. Music and dance were a lifeline for those thousands of miles away from everything they knew and loved. This is why dance is such an essential part of identity and connection to stories and people.

DADA'S STORY

Dada and my eldest uncle

My paternal grandfather Mohammed Nasim Khan, or Dada grew up in Saharanpur, North India, and was born in 1906! That's over a hundred years ago, and I still cannot get my head around that and my direct connection to a bygone era. He sadly died when I was still a baby.

Dada was a revolutionary and extremely principled; he did not follow the crowd. He pursued a formal education, and then made sure that his five sons and two daughters were all educated to a high standard. They are a family of PhDs, medical doctors and post graduates. This was rare in Indian society at that time for Muslims, especially for Muslim women. He believed this was the real essence of Islam; equality of men and women.

Dada was a police inspector and my dad used to tell us fascinating stories of how Dada met historical figures in pre-Partition India, including Muhammad Iqbal, Jinnah, Nehru and Gandhi. These accounts drew me into this period of history which I consequently ended up studying at university. Dada loved poetry, especially poets of the Indian sub-continent, like Muhammad Iqbal.

Dada refused to leave India, not because he did not believe in Pakistan, but because he did not want to leave behind his fellow Muslims who may have been in danger through communal violence. As a police inspector, he was in a position of authority and out of principle, he stayed behind. His sacrifice to stay behind in India, for the sake of others was a noble act, one that we are all proud of.

Sadly, the Muslims in India are currently suffering under the Islamophobic government, and they are threatened with eradication because of their faith. It is extremely difficult to obtain visas to visit my family in India because of my

• Kathak dancer

Pakistani heritage and the fact that I was born there. These are the sad realities of Partition that we live with every day and have a huge impact on our lives.

INDO-PAKISTAN'S VIBRANT DANCE CULTURE

People are often surprised to learn that Pakistan, the land of cricket, parathas and ladoo, has a rich but hidden dance tradition.

Dance styles are plentiful across all regions of this vast country, and include a beautiful variety of folk as well as classical dance. The dance forms and their stories are inextricably linked with India. Although the subcontinent was physically divided in 1947, the butchery of the British carving knife was not able to sever a connection that goes back for millennia.

Nighat Chaudhry, a Pakistani professional dancer now based in Lahore, has been one of the main proponents of kathak classical dance in Pakistan. She grew up in the UK and studied contemporary dance and ballet, but after learning from a Pakistani dancer and discovering her own cultural dance heritage, she never looked back. Nighat found her calling to return to Pakistan, immerse herself in the dance and preserve the hidden art form for the nation.

Nighat has been practising classical kathak dance since she was 13 years old. She says, "Sadly, dance has been heavily politicised in Pakistan. It used to be more vibrant and open, but for several decades now we seem to have lost the acceptance of dance as a spiritual expression. Dance has been a breakthrough for me personally. Through dance I found myself, and within myself, I found God."

In the early days of the creation of Pakistan, there seems to have been a more tolerant attitude towards dance and performing arts. In 1966, Pakistan International Airlines (PIA) established an Arts Academy to positively promote the culture of Pakistan. The Arts Academy was very prominent in its day, and the well-known actor and performer, Zia Mohyeddin, was appointed Director from 1937 to 1977. He married Nahid Siddiqui, a famous Pakistani kathak dancer, she brought her own style of Sufi and spiritual aesthetics to this classical dance. Nahid Siddiqui immersed herself in Islamic principles and geometry to further develop her kathak movements, poses and body alignment. My family would host the Pakistan Arts Academy on their visits to the UK, and were privileged to witness their performances in close-knit family gatherings at my grandparents' home in Central London.

The direction of travel for the acceptance of dance in Pakistan began to change in the late 1970s and 1980s, when dance was actually banned by the government. Unfortunately, this led to a stagnation and decline of the practice at a formal level. Outside Pakistan, many would presume that there is no dance heritage in Pakistan which could not be further from the truth.

Despite the strict edicts from those in power, it has proven difficult to eradicate dance. Pakistanis continue to dance, with folk dances being extremely popular. "Folk dancing is very vibrant in Pakistan," says Nighat. "We have community folk dances including bhangra, balochi and lewa to name a few. These dances tend to have more gender mixing as it's normally a family affair, and it's inclusive."

Where there are people, there is always a presence of dance and movement, even when governments try to suppress or ban it. In Pakistan, dance is used for rituals, communal activity and celebrations such as weddings, but also by Sufis in a spiritual and devotional context. Sufism is very popular in both Pakistan and India as it is in neighbouring Muslim countries. This Sufi heritage is a result of the traditions that Indian Muslim rulers brought with them from Central Asia and Persia. The Mughals were very Sufi in their outlook, and patronised many Sufi saints and scholars. The Sufism practised in Pakistan is steeped in this heritage, and it is part and parcel of the fabric of society, including poetry, literature and music.

Traditional Indian classical dance also permeates dance forms in Pakistan, but it is not patronised or promoted. Nighat believes that kathak dance or Bharatnatyam seems to be the most contentious dance forms in Pakistan due to their obvious links with India. Nighat is adamant that there is more to the non-acceptance of dance in Pakistan than mere religious grounds. It's true that certain orthodox elements of society believe dance is not allowed in Islam; however, that is not everyone's view. The real barrier seems to be more political in nature and based on deep trauma from Partition, also a drive to develop a completely different culture and existence to India. Nighat says, "The establishment have not wanted any connection to India at all, including through dance. Though I hope that in the future this might change, but maybe not in my lifetime."

The irony is that kathak is deeply rooted in Indian Muslim history, and is in fact an Indo-Muslim Persian dance style. The present form of kathak dance is a beautiful fusion of indigenous Indian tradition with Muslim culture that was prevalent in the northern parts of India, during the golden age of the Mughal Empire, from the sixteenth to eighteenth century.

Islamic rulers in India were admirers of many aspects of pre-Islamic Indian culture. They therefore incorporated kathak - a north Indian classical storytelling tradition through dance - and adapted it into their own cultural traditions. Many of kathak's elements stem from an older local Hindu tradition. However, in its aesthetics, as well as some of its technical aspects characterised by linear poses and pirouettes, kathak clearly reflects the Islamic influences, to a great extent, from Persia.

The period of British colonial rule sent kathak into decline. Kathak was still practised in its original courtly context, but the British regarded it as low entertainment and gave it an unwholesome image by calling it 'nauch dance', meaning 'prostitute's dance', more or less.

While kathak now thrives in India on the other side of the border, it is sadly not patronised. Pakistan's rejection of this classical style also means a rejection of a large part of its own history and identity. Sufi dancing is probably the most accepted dance form in Pakistan due to the popularity of Sufism and its connection to spirituality.

Nighat herself believes in the power of dance to impact spiritual healing. She says, "I run my own dance institute and also teach dance therapy courses. I strongly believe in the power of dance to have healing powers, and I promote using Sufi dance practices and movement therapy to help those suffering mentally and emotionally. There is so much more to dance than the linear view of its connection to immorality. There are many layers, and it has the power to uplift people, tell stories and convey a community's rich heritage."

As Pakistan's reputation grows as a centre of culture and heritage, thanks to a younger generation of YouTubers and travellers, perhaps Nighat's hopes may come true sooner than anticipated. It is her wish that Pakistan's rich dance history is recognised, and that there will be immense value in embracing the art form and its connected stories in years to come.

BHANGRA

Bhangra dance is a shared heritage of the Punjab area and is practised by both Muslims and Sikhs. Since Partition, part of Punjab is in India but the majority of the region is in Pakistan.

The origins of bhangra can be traced back at least two thousand years, starting in the Sialkot area of Pakistan. Like other dance forms I have explored, it started off as movements focused around working, harvesting the land and nature. Interestingly, one of the harvested products, bhang (hemp) lends its name to the now world-famous bhangra dance.

The accompanying music and lyrics are called 'boliyan' and are short songs played to the beat of the dhol drum. It is an energetic dance with jumping, leaping, leg kicks, arm movements, twists and turns. There are different forms of bhangra including the Jhumar, Luddi, Giddha, Julli, Daankara, Saami and Kikli which are all from different regions of the Punjab.

Whilst bhangra is generally associated with the Sikh community in India, it is often forgotten that it is a shared heritage with Muslims in Pakistan. This is mainly due to the fact that Muslim dance is less known in general and not promoted in the same manner. At Pakistani weddings and parties, bhangra is often a core part of music and dance celebrations.

GATKA STICK DANCE

Gatka, also known as Dandiya, is a popular martial arts style dance practised in Khyber Pakhtunwala and surrounding areas, as well as areas of Punjab. Dancers use wooden sticks and enter into a mock sword dance.

The dance is traditionally passed on from older family members but can also be learned in formal settings where available. There is some dispute as to where the dance style originated; some say it was from the Sikh community and others say it began from the times of the Mughals. Either way, it is a dance that is popular across Sikh communities and Muslim communities in areas of Pakistan.

16- Long History of Islam in the Far East

Islam arrived in the Far East quite early on in its history and was primarily brought to these lands by Arab traders.

The first Muslim to have arrived in China, according to traditional Chinese Muslim accounts, was Sa'd ibn Abi Waqqas, a close companion of the Prophet Muhammad. He is believed to have arrived in Canton (Guangzhou) in 627 CE, and visited again many more times. In 651 CE, Sa'd was sent by Caliph Uthman and granted an audience with the Tang Emperor, Gaozong, who received the envoy. The Emperor ordered the construction of a mosque in Canton and the city is known as one of the first Muslim settlements in China.

• Kinding Sindaw, Filipino Muslim Dance Theatre Company

Through trade, more and more Muslims ventured along the Silk Road to China and many settled there, marrying with the local population. Numerous Muslims migrated to China during the Yuan Dynasty (1271-1368), where they were called to work as administrators for the rulers who were descendants of the Mongols. As the Mongols had a great deal of connections with Muslims along the Silk Road, they trusted their skills in bureaucracy.

Muslims are still present in China, many from the time of the early Muslim migration and are indigenous to the land. Although they are still a minority and make up less than two per cent of the population, they are an officially recognised community. Out of fifty-six ethnic groupings recognised in China, ten of these are Muslims, including Hui, Uyghur, Kazakh, Dongxiang, Kyrgyz, Salar, Tajik, Uzbek, Bonan and Tatar. Even though they may share the same Chinese ethnicity as the rest of the population, Muslims are discriminated against because of their faith. Other countries in the present-day Far East have majority Muslim populations such as Indonesia, which has 87 per cent[164] Muslim inhabitants and Malaysia, which has 61 per cent.[165]

Arab traders ventured to the Indonesian archipelago due to trade and to pick up rare spices, which were found on these lands. This started as early as the eighth century, but large numbers of Muslim traders settled here permanently from the thirteenth century. From this time, there were significant Muslim communities, which has been verified in the writings of Ibn Battuta and Marco Polo. Historian, Dr Carrol Kersten, says, "First evidences of the local people converting to Islam in present-day Indonesia does not date further than the 13th century. That's when we find ground archaeological evidence, namely tombstones of sultans with Arab names, which demonstrate that local leaders have embraced Islam (sic)."[166]

The settlers practised their faith but did not impose it on the native population. Gradually, some rulers adopted the religion of Islam and it consequently spread through the ruling classes. A fusion of cultures was created, and many people embraced the religion out of their own accord and through intermarriage.

Islam increased in a similar way in Malaysia and other South East Asian lands including Brunei and the Southern Philippines. The spread of the religion was natural and syncretic. The practice of Sufism that was brought with the traders established strong roots in the Far East, and this had an immense influence on the locals, especially in the early days of Islam. The more orthodox interpretations of Islam started to make inroads in the Far East from the 1900s onwards. This challenged the syncretism that existed here for hundreds of years.

The dance of the Southern Philippines demonstrates the fusion of cultures, including the indigenous and Islamic. Muslim dance in the Philippines is well known across the Islands for its distinct style. The performance is a very visual affair with traditional Muslim clothing, props such as bamboo sticks and fans, and facial and bodily expressions. The dance is also practised by Muslims in the diaspora where the customs are being kept alive and passed on to younger generations.

KINDING SINDAW: MUSLIM DANCE TROUPE FROM SOUTHERN PHILIPPINES

A New York based, Muslim-run dance troupe recreates the ancient traditions of the Mindanao people of southern Philippines, with the aim of preserving the people, ancient heritage and beautiful oral history.

Founder Potri Ranka Morris started 'Kinding Sindaw' in 1992. The name means 'A Spark of Graceful Movement' which relates to both dance and conscious-based action. Potri is from the Southern Philippines, a Muslim majority population located mainly on the island of Mindanao and still very much a tribal community. Potri's tribe back in the Philippines, are known for their skills as artists and storytellers. The stories of these tribal people and their oral history is told through the practice of dance, poetry and song.

Setting up Kinding Sindaw is part of Potri's life purpose and loyalty towards her tribe. The organisation is her passion, and it is driven by an altruistic goal of preserving the people and heritage of the Southern Philippines. "The people are facing the danger of extinction due to their minority Muslim status and the government's incursion into their lands," says Potri. "We are here to keep the ancient tradition alive but also to educate, raise consciousness and create a call to action. We want audiences to raise the issue of the South Philippines people to our government and help stop the destruction of a community." According to an article by a Christian priest, Lakan Sumulong, "Muslims in southern Philippines... are still living under deteriorating political, economic, and social conditions."[167] He adds that the government is failing to protect Muslim ancestral lands.

The Philippines is a cluster of 7,600 Islands in South Asia that sits between Indonesia, Malaysia, and China. It has indigenous animist beliefs with influences from Hinduism and Buddhism. Muslims ruled most of the Philippines from the thirteenth to sixteenth century and brought the Islamic faith, Arabic language and cultural traditions. The Spanish conquered it in the sixteenth century, and the land was called 'the Philippines' after King Phillip II of Spain. Most of the country became Catholic, but Southern Spain remained majority Muslim and they now make up five per cent of the total population of the Philippines.

The indigenous people followed a way of life closely connected to the natural environment. There are a lot of cultural practices from Hinduism. Potri's name, for example, is from Sanskrit (an ancient Indian language) and means daughter. Dance is also a very important part of Hindu tradition, and there are similarities in Filipino culture of using dance to connect with nature and tell stories.

When Islam arrived in the Philippines, the rulers did not wipe out these existing traditions but perhaps Islamised them or made them less polytheistic. Potri says, "We were able to keep our traditions because of Islam." In the Spanish-ruled parts of the country, many of the ancient traditions were wiped out because Spanish rulers brought Christianity and Spanish cultural domination. "Islamic rulers didn't eradicate the culture that was already there. It brought its language (Arabic), cultures and traditions and these integrated into indigenous practices including dance and storytelling," says Potri. As with many Muslim empires throughout history, you often see the merging of indigenous traditions with the cultural practices brought by the Muslim rulers, creating the most beautiful and unique art and culture that still exists to this day.

The Southern Philippines remained Muslim and did not fall to the Spanish because the Muslims fought strongly to protect their way of life and religious freedoms. They were expert swordsmen and fighters. They practised a martial arts form, that is also common in Malaysia and Indonesia, called Silat. The religion also united the various tribes in the south and they became a strong force of resistance. According to Filipino historian, Renato Constantino, the Muslim South was never fully conquered, "By virtue of its higher social and economic development and its better organized and more tenacious resistance."[168]

After all these years of Southern Filipino tradition being preserved, the fear that exists now is that these beautiful ancient customs will be wiped out by the government wanting to assimilate the population, implement modernisation and corporate capitalism. The dances performed by Kinding Sindaw are a living tradition that have been passed down from generation to generation since ancient times. These are ritual dances of tribes that still exist. One of the most famous dances of the Mindanao people is known as the Singkil. It's a story of a princess who gets lost in the forest, and a prince comes to rescue her. The dance involves fans and large bamboo poles which are weaved in and out close to the floor trying to trip up the princess. The dancer must display incredible footwork and grace to avoid the poles. Potri says, "If you want this dance to be preserved, you have to preserve the people. It is our obligation to raise these serious issues as we are in a privileged position living with the freedoms we have."

It is very true that diversity of people and cultures is what makes the world so beautiful and rich. Preserving these stories and dance forms are important for the whole world, and once destroyed, are forever lost. "We can't have a generation of people who don't know their roots. The only way to be grounded and have a purpose is to know where you came from," says Potri.

It is uplifting to hear that cultural dance forms, such as those practised by Muslims in the South Philippines, still exist today. We must support groups like Kinding Sindaw to spread the beauty, but also the important message of preserving cultural heritage.

Conclusion— Reclaiming our Dance History

The purpose of this book was to show that dance and movement exist in abundance across the Muslim world and consequently across Muslim diaspora communities. It was also to show the connection between folk dance and spirituality, and the role that Sufism played in creating movement that was primarily about 'Tawhid' or the Oneness of God. There are many dance styles and areas across the Muslim world that are not covered either because the information was lacking or they did not fall into the Silk Road region. This is just the beginning of this discussion and there is definitely more detailed work that can be done in this field.

Dance is a vital link to our past, and all the wondrous varieties bind together the stories of our communities throughout time. The movements and music help us understand the people, landscape and their connection to nature and spirituality. To deny Muslim dance is to deny our very existence.

Dance is far from being non-existent in the Muslim world or overly sexualised as is the mainstream perception; however, sadly, it does not receive its due attention because of the plentiful reasons which I have highlighted throughout this book. These include certain orthodox views from within the Muslim community, the destruction of our history and heritage at the hands of colonialism, as well as cultural appropriation in the West. The latter has, in turn, corrupted Muslim dance forms to fit into Orientalist fantasies and views of the East.

In fact, traditional dance in the Muslim world portrays something more than aesthetics alone, and that is a connection to the soul of Islam. Across Muslim lands, there is very much a shared Islamic culture which stems from the core essence of the religion and its teachings. Concepts of Tawhid, the connection to nature, Zakat (charity), hospitality, Ilm (knowledge) are some of the principles that connect the Muslims worldwide. We are a multicultural and diverse community that share unbreakable bonds that bypass man-made boundaries and nation states. These shared elements have influenced the development of culture, including dance, across the Muslim world. Professor Omid Safi states, "Islamic art and literature are not simply the illustration or ornamentation of mundane material, nor even a way of sacralizing and beautifying a medium with Islamic aesthetic. In their highest form, they can be a portal that open up subtle mysteries from the heart of the Islamic tradition."[169]

Spirituality and connection with the Divine are present in many folk dances and not only in specific Sufi spiritual dances, such as that of the Whirling Dervishes. The inspiration for folk dance comes from nature, creation, working the land and day-to-day activities, which in Muslim societies historically would all be linked to God. The dances that have developed consequently are beautiful, graceful and deep in meaning. Even where dance is now used as a tool for political activism and resistance, this too is linked to the concept of justice in Islam.

The elements that make up the dance including the clothing, lyrics of the sung poetry written by Sufi teachers, how genders interact in the dance, and the stories that are being told through movement, incorporate Islamic norms and traditions. It is therefore imperative to remove the connotations of traditional dance being the same as that found in modern-day night clubs around the Muslim world.

In addition to Islamic spirituality, dance across the Silk Road was influenced by the dominant Central Asian, Turkic, Persian and Arabic cultures that ruled powerful empires in these lands. These aforementioned traditions and people have intermingled so closely since the advent of Islam due to regular interaction along the Silk Road that, practically created an amalgamated culture across the whole trade route.

Muslim empires at their height were dynamic, innovative and wealthy and as a result were envied by the Western world who tried desperately for centuries to catch up. Some Muslim rulers across the Silk Road patronised culture and heritage, including music and dance. Under their leadership, arts flourished and dance styles were fused with local practices including Shamanism, Buddhism and Animism–so long as they did not conflict with Islamic teachings. This led to a continuation of the story that came before them, merging their new ways with existing heritage.

The power and influence of the Muslim Empires, at their height, was admired in the West, and the arts and culture coming from the East was copied, though the aesthetics often became removed from their spiritual essence. It is also important to remember that Islam has been part of Europe for hundreds of years. As a result, Islamic cultural influences have permeated Western culture to this day, and the evidence is in plain sight to those who are aware of the history and connections with the East.

European dances like flamenco have been influenced by Andalusian Muslim dance culture, alongside local Spanish, Gypsy and Jewish cultures as they all lived together under almost eight hundred years of Muslim rule in Spain. Some also believe that Moorish dancing is said to have influenced Morris dancing in Britain. Writer, Rodney Gallop, said, "It had, of course, never been questioned that the name 'Morris' was a corruption of the word 'Morisco' and it had been generally believed that the dance was in fact of Moorish origin."[170]

The history of dance, alongside the study of other arts and culture, is crucial in understanding people and their identities. Even now in the diaspora, people hold firmly onto their culture as it is a link to where they come from.

Dance is a strong part of this connection. From the nineteenth century, as empires began to split up into countries with borders and boundaries, dance was one of the tools used by nation builders to rally the population around a shared narrative. Dance continues to play this role in the diaspora, and to bring people together when they are far away from home. It also important to reflect on the shared dance histories that still exist across manmade borders, which connect rather than divide us.

ENDNOTES

1 Surah Al-Hujurat, Verse 13, Qur'an; translation Abdul Haleem

2 Sonia Hinz, "Dance, Mysticism, and Sensuality Perspectives from Tajikistan"; A thesis submitted to the graduate division of the university of Hawaii in partial fulfilment of the requirements for the degree of Master of Arts in Dance; May 2007, p. 57.

3 John Martin as cited in Judith R. Mackrell: Performing Arts; https://www.britannica.com/art/dance

4 Lois Ibsen al Faruqi, Dance as an Expression of Islamic Culture in Dance Research Journal , Spring - Summer, 1978, Vol. 10, No. 2 (Spring - Summer, 1978), p. 6.

5 Ibid., p. 12.

6 Ibid., p. 12.

7 Modern in this context is post nineteenth century

8 Dr Laurel Victoria Gray, The Silk Road Dance of Feminine Deity: An Interview with Laurel Victoria Gray by B. Claire; http://www.laurelvictoriagray.com/silk-road-dance-of-feminine-deity.html.

9 Knowledge of Islam and Muslims crystallised into what became known, by the late 18th century, as Orientalism—the study of the history, languages and cultures of the East—Roger Hardy. It is now often used with negative connotations of a colonialist bias underlying and reinforced by such scholarship. As cited in Merriam-Webster dictionary https://www.merriam-webster.com/dictionary/Orientalism

10 Recep Dogan, "The Soul's Need to Connect with God through the Language of Art: Analysis from an Islamic Perspective"; (Wisdom College, Brisbane, Australia; 27 February 2018)

11 Art for art's sake, a slogan translated from the French l'art pour l'art, which was coined in the early 19th century. The phrase expresses the belief held by many writers and artists, especially those associated with Astheticism that art needs no justification, that it need serve no political, didactic r other end. As cited in Britannica online, https://www.britannica.com/topic/art-for-arts-sake

12 Sonia Hinz, "Dance, Mysticism, and Sensuality Perspectives from Tajikistan"; A thesis submitted to the graduate division of the university of Hawaii in partial fulfilment of the requirements for the degree of Master of

Arts in Dance; May 2007, p. 70.
13 Sefik Can, "Fundamentals of Rumi's Thought: A Mevlevi Sufi Perspective"; (New Jersey: The Light, 2005), p.203
14 Hadiths are a collection of traditions and sayings of the Prophet Muhammad
15 Sefik Can, "Fundamentals of Rumi's Thought: A Mevlevi Sufi Perspective"; (New Jersey: The Light, 2005), p.208
16 Sonia Hinz, "Dance, Mysticism, and Sensuality Perspectives from Tajikistan"; A thesis submitted to the graduate division of the university of Hawaii in partial fulfilment of the requirements for the degree of Master of Arts in Dance; May 2007, p.12
17 Camille Helminski, Women of Sufism, A Hidden Treasure (Shambhala, 2003), p. 125-126
18 Dr Laurel Gray, The Silk Road Dance of Feminine Deity: An Interview with Laurel Victoria Gray by B. Claire; http://www.laurelvictoriagray.com/silk-road-dance-of-feminine-deity.html
19 A. Reza Hoshmand, Eurasian Connection via the Silk Road: The Spread of Islam; https://www.researchgate.net/publication/329349354_Eurasian_Connection_via_the_Silk_Road_The_Spread_of_Islam_Reinventing_the_Past_and_Shaping_the_Future
20 Peter Frankopan, The Silk Roads by: A New History of the Worlds; (Bloomsbury, London, New York, 2015 (The Libraries Consortium)), p.173.
21 Peter Frankopan, The Silk Roads by: A New History of the Worlds; (Bloomsbury, London, New York, 2015 (The Libraries Consortium)) p.152.
22 Ibid., p.154.
23 Ibid., p.181.
24 Cherif Bassiouni, Introduction to Islam; https://www.mei.edu/publications/introduction-islam#7
25 The Qu'ran; Surah Al-Hujarat, (49:13)
26 Akbar S. Ahmed, Discovering Islam: making sense of Muslim history and society; (Revised edition; Routledge, 1988, 2002), p.44.
27 A term not coined until the late 19th century; a political ideology advocating unity of Muslims
28 Cherif Bassiouni, Introduction to Islam; https://www.mei.edu/publications/introduction-islam#7
29 Ibid.

30 Ibid.
31 Akbar S. Ahmed, Discovering Islam: making sense of Muslim history and society; (Revised edition; Routledge, 1988, 2002), p. 228.
32 Peter Frankopan, The Silk Roads by: A New History of the Worlds; (Bloomsbury, London, New York, 2015 (The Libraries Consortium)), p. 64.
33 Ibid., p. 66.
34 Ibid p. 78.
35 Lisa Traiger, Movement along the Silk Road, June 2002; https://www.washingtonpost.com/archive/lifestyle/2002/06/21/movement-along-the-silk-road/27243066-b60b-485a-a49d-e8d23ee6015a/
36 NOTE: I am using 'sema' as the spelling for the Whirling Dervish Ceremony, whereas it has many different spellings, and Annemarie Schimmel uses 'sam'a'.
37 Annemarie Schimmel, Mystical Dimensions of Islam (The University of North Carolina Press, Chapel Hill; 1975), p.179.
38 Ibid., p. 317.
39 Ibid., p179
40 Ibid., 179
41 Seyyed Hossein Nasr, interviewed on Sami Yusuf's 'Reflections'; YouTube https://youtu.be/N8Ii_BANqSk From 30:31
42 Ibid., From 30:53
43 Ibid., From 34:12
44 Annemarie Schimmel, Mystical Dimensions of Islam (The University of North Carolina Press, Chapel Hill; 1975), p.406
45 Ibid., p. 240.
46 Ibid., p. 346.
47 Ibid., p.406
48 Bruce Miller, Rumi Comes to America: How the Poet of Mystical Love Arrived on our Shores (Miller eMedia; 2nd ed. (November 21, 2018), p.35
49 Ibid., p. 35
50 Jason Webster, Andalus: Unlocking the Secrets of Moorish Spain (Doubleday: 2004), p. 64.
51 Ana Ruiz, Vibrant Andalusia: The Spice of Life in Southern Spain (Algora Publishing: 2007), p.7.
52 Jason Webster, Andalus: Unlocking the Secrets of Moorish Spain (Doubleday: 2004), p. 90.
53 Ana Ruiz, Vibrant Andalusia: The Spice of Life in Southern Spain

(Algora Publishing: 2007), p. 42.
54 Medina Tenour Whiteman, Flamenco: A Gypsy-Andalusian Love Affair, https://alandalus-experience.com/flamenco-a-gypsy-andalusian-love-affair/
55 Ana Ruiz, Vibrant Andalusia: The Spice of Life in Southern Spain (Algora Publishing: 2007), p. 33.
56 Ibid., p. 42.
57 Medina Tenour Whiteman, Flamenco: A Gypsy-Andalusian Love Affair, https://alandalus-experience.com/flamenco-a-gypsy-andalusian-love-affair/
58 Ana Ruiz, Vibrant Andalusia: The Spice of Life in Southern Spain (Algora Publishing: 2007) p. 54.
59 Ibid., p. 55.
60 Ibid., p. 61.
61 Medina Tenour Whiteman, Flamenco: A Gypsy-Andalusian Love Affair, https://alandalus-experience.com/flamenco-a-gypsy-andalusian-love-affair/
62 Historians dispute Ziryab's exact ethnicity. He was believed to be either Kurdish, Persian or African
63 Ana Ruiz, Vibrant Andalusia: The Spice of Life in Southern Spain (Algora Publishing: 2007), p. 32.
64 Ibid., p. 28.
65 Suraiya Faroqhi, Subjects of the Sultan: Culture and Daily Life in the Ottoman Empire, (I.B. Tauris, London, New York; 2005), p. 80.
66 An elite military force for the Ottoman Empire, made up of child slaves. Many went on to hold very high ranks and power
67 Arzu Ozturkmen, Modern Dance "Alla Turca:" Transforming Ottoman Dance in Early Republican Turkey Author(s): as cited in Dance Research Journal , Summer, 2003, Vol. 35, No. 1 (Summer, 2003), pp. 38-60.
68 Ibid., p.46
69 Arzu Ozturkmen, Politics of National Dance in Turkey: A Historical Reappraisal: in Yearbook for Traditional Music, Vol. 33 (2001); p.139
70 Ibid., p.140
71 Ibid., p.142
72 Ibid., p.142
73 Leyla Hammefendi, as cited in 'Turkish Orientale Belly Dance'; https://babayagamusic.com/Encyclopedic-Dictionary-Ethnic-Arts/turkish-oriental-belly-dance.htm

74 A letter written by Lady Mary Wortley Montagu in 1718; https://pressbooks.pub/pacbl1/chapter/from-the-letters-of-lady-mary-wortley-montagu/#:~:text=I%20am%20well%2Dacquainted%20with,repent%20the%20choice%20he%20made
75 Arzu Ozturkmen, Modern Dance "Alla Turca:" Transforming Ottoman Dance in Early Republican Turkey Author(s): as cited in Dance Research Journal , Summer, 2003, Vol. 35, No. 1 (Summer, 2003), pp. 38- 60.
76 Theodore Barber, Four Interpretations of Mevlevi Dervish Dance, 1920-1929; Dance Chronicle , 1986, Vol. 9, No. 3 (1986), (Taylor & Francis, Ltd.) pp. 328-355.
77 Ibid.
78 Anthony Shay, The Zeybek,; https://www.rem.routledge.com/articles/zeybek-the
79 Anadalou Agency; https://www.dailysabah.com/history/2015/12/03/ottoman-folk-dance-promotes-peace-around-the-world
80 Holy Qur'an: (2:256)
81 Tharik Hussain, Minarets in the Mountains: A Journey into Muslim Europe; (Bradt, 2021), p.65.
82 Ibid., p.312
83 Ayse Osmanoglu, The Gilded Cage on the Bosphorus: The Ottomans: The Story of a Family; (Hanedan Press, 2020), p. 30.
84 How Balkan 'folk dances' are made – "Arranged Folklore"; https://folkdancefootnotes.org/begin/how-balkan-folk-dances-are-made-arranged-folklore/
85 Tharik Hussain, Minarets in the Mountains: A Journey into Muslim Europe; (Bradt, 2021), p.30.
86 Ibid. p.21
87 Esma Kucukalic, The House of the Open Door: From Ibn Arabi to Al Bosnevi. The Mediterranean Sufism That Took Root in the Balkans; https://www.iemed.org/publication/the-house-of-the-open-door-from-ibn-arabi-to-al-bosnevi-the-mediterranean-sufism-that-took-root-in-the-balkans/
88 Ibid.
89 Tamara Karača-Beljak, Jasmina Talam, Ottoman Influence on Folk Music Tradition of Bosnia and Herzegovina (University of Sarajevo, 2015)
90 Nicolae Roddy (ed.), Religious History and Culture of the Balkans,; Journal of Religion and Society, Supplement 19 (2019)

91 Tamara Karača-Beljak, Jasmina Talam, Ottoman Influence on Folk Music Tradition of Bosnia and Herzegovina (University of Sarajevo, 2015)
92 Nicolae Roddy (ed.), Religious History and Culture of the Balkans,; Journal of Religion and Society, Supplement 19 (2019))
93 Dr Stef Keris: History of Islam in Russia; https://youtu.be/ANl7I-zi9e2E?si=Ihp6g9gltnATHeGq
94 As cited in the Moscow Times; https://www.themoscowtimes.com/2018/06/01/your-primer-on-tatar-culture-a61907
95 As cited in Wikipedia; https://en.wikipedia.org/wiki/Rudolf_Nureyev#:~:text=In%20his%20autobiography%2C%20Nureyev%20noted,relatives%20are%20Tatars%20and%20Bashkirs.
96 Takutdinova Diana, Islamic Reflection in Tatar Folk Dance; Master's Thesis in Choreomundus, International Master in Dance Knowledge, Practice, and Heritage; (Spring 2017), p.19
97 Ibid. p. 12.
98 Ibid. p. 18.
99 Ibid. p. 52.
100 Ibid. p. 63.
101 As cited in the Moscow Times; https://www.themoscowtimes.com/2018/06/01/your-primer-on-tatar-culture-a61907
102 Razia Sultanova, From Shamanism to Sufism: Women, Islam and Culture in Central Asia (I.B. Taurus, 2014), pp. 4-5.
103 Ibid., p. 5.
104 Peter Frankopan, The Silk Roads by: A New History of the Worlds; (Bloomsbury, London, New York, 2015 (The Libraries Consortium)); p.155
105 Ibid., p.154.
106 Tara Pandeya as cited in: https://voicesoncentralasia.org/sweat-blood-and-central-asian-dance/
107 Ibid.
108 Sonia Hinz, "Dance, Mysticism, and Sensuality Perspectives from Tajikistan"; A thesis submitted to the graduate division of the university of Hawaii in partial fulfilment of the requirements for the degree of Master of Arts in Dance; May 2007; p.153.
109 Ibid. p. 63.
110 Ibid. p. 70.
111 Razia Sultanova, From Shamanism to Sufism: Women, Islam and Culture in Central Asia (I.B. Taurus, 2014), p.27.

112 Tara Pandeya as cited in: https://voicesoncentralasia.org/sweat-blood-and-central-asian-dance/
113 As cited in, Razia Sultanova, From Shamanism to Sufism: Women, Islam and Culture in Central Asia (I.B. Taurus, 2014), p. 21.
114 Tara Pandeya as cited in: https://voicesoncentralasia.org/sweat-blood-and-central-asian-dance/
115 Professor Alexander Djumaev, as cited in https://voicesoncentralasia.org/shashmaqam-music-and-poetry-of-central-asia/
116 Sonia Hinz, "Dance, Mysticism, and Sensuality Perspectives from Tajikistan"; A thesis submitted to the graduate division of the university of Hawaii in partial fulfilment of the requirements for the degree of Master of Arts in Dance; May 2007, p.162.
117 Professor Alexander Djumaev, as cited in https://voicesoncentralasia.org/shashmaqam-music-and-poetry-of-central-asia/
118 Ibid.
119 Ibid.
120 Ibid.
121 Ibid.
122 Ibid.
123 Sonia Hinz, "Dance, Mysticism, and Sensuality Perspectives from Tajikistan"; A thesis submitted to the graduate division of the university of Hawaii in partial fulfilment of the requirements for the degree of Master of Arts in Dance; May 2007; p. 35.
124 Khan Bahadur was the title of respect and honour given by the British gave to Muslim natives of British India
125 Dr Rachel Harris and Yasin Mahpul; Uyghur National Congress; https://www.uyghurcongress.org/en/uyghur-music/
126 Rachel Harris as cited in: http://www.meshrep.uk/the-uyghur-meshrep-a-traditional-community-gathering-censored-in-china/
127 Ibid.
128 Mark Hay; Islamic Sexology, https://aeon.co/essays/islam-has-a-long-tradition-of-explicit-sexual-discussion
129 Anthony Shay and Barbara Sellers-Young; Belly Dance: Orientalism: Exoticism: Self-Exoticism; Dance Research Journal, Summer 2003, Vol. 35, No. 1 (Summer 2003), pp 13-37.
130 Mark Hay; Islamic Sexology, https://aeon.co/essays/islam-has-a-long-tradition-of-explicit-sexual-discussion
131 Anthony Shay and Barbara Sellers-Young; Belly Dance: Orientalism:

Exoticism: Self-Exoticism; Dance Research Journal, Summer 2003, Vol. 35, No. 1 (Summer 2003), p.16

132 Daniel Otero, History of the belly dance: is it to entice men or a female's rite of passage? Shenzhen Guangming Foreign Languages School, China; Arts and Humanity Open Access Journal; Volume 4 Issue 5 - 2020 https://medcraveonline.com/AHOAJ/AHOAJ-04-00171.pdf

133 Ibid.

134 Ibid.

135 Ibid.

136 Michelle Harper; as cited in: https://www.readex.com/blog/hoochie-coochie-lure-forbidden-belly-dance-victorian-america

137 Shayna Silverstein, Syria's Radical Dabka, Middle East Report , Summer 2012, No. 263, THE ART & CULTURE OF THE ARAB REVOLTS (Summer 2012); Middle East Research and Information Project, Inc. (MERIP), pp. 33-37.

138 Ibid.

139 Ibid.

140 Mehr Afshan Farooqi, Ghalib: A Wildenrness at My Doorstep: A Critical Biography (Allen Lane, 2021), p.437

141 Anthony Shay, Dance and Non-Dance: Patterned Movement in Iran and Islam; Iranian Studies, (Winter - Spring, 1995, Vol. 28, No. 1/2 (Winter - Spring, 1995), Taylor & Francis, Ltd. on behalf of International Society of Iranian Studies): https://www.jstor.org/stable/4310918; pp. 61-78.

142 Nilla Cram Cook, The Theater and Ballet Arts of Iran, (Middle East Journal, Oct., 1949, Vol. 3, No. 4 (Oct., 1949)); Middle East Institute; https://www.jstor.org/stable/4322114 pp. 406-420.

143 Arezou Azad, The Beginnings of Islam in Afghanistan: Conquest, Acculturation, and Islamization; https://content.ucpress.edu/chapters/13363.ch01.pdf

144 Nile Green, Afghanistan's Islam; From Conversion to the Taliban, (Ed.) Nile Green; (University of California Press); p.5

145 Ibid., p.10

146 Ibid., p.12

147 Nushin Arbabzadah, Women and Religious Patronage in the Timurid Empire in Afghanistan's Islam; From Conversion to the Taliban, (Ed.) Nile Green; (University of California Press); https://www.degruyter.com/document/doi/10.1515/9780520967373-007/html?lang=en&srsltid=AfmBOor_50iwv9yj3Ii_xerMGkgmO3gS5uQ9zZSjCOGWj8Y6OYP08agb

p.65
148 Nile Green, Afghanistan's Islam A History and It's Scholarship, (University of California Press), https://muse.jhu.edu/pub/263/oa_monograph/chapter/2260119/pdf p.12
149 Ehsan Bayat, A Look at the Fascinating World of Traditional Afghan Dance; https://ehsanbayatafghanwireless.com/look-fascinating-world-traditional-afghan-dance/
150 Dhol: a double-headed barrel drum
151 Nushin Arbabzadah, Women and Religious Patronage in the Timurid Empire in Afghanistan's Islam; From Conversion to the Taliban, (Ed.) Nile Green; (University of California Press); https://www.degruyter.com/document/doi/10.1515/9780520967373-007/html?lang=en&srsltid=AfmBOor_50iwv9yj3Ii_xerMGkgmO3gS5uQ9zZSjCOGWj8Y6OYP08agb p.57
152 Ibid. p.60
153 William Dalrymple, The Anarchy: The Relentless Rise of the East India Company; (Bloomsbury Publishing; 2020), p.xxxiii
154 Ibid., p. 18.
155 Audrey Truschke, Aurangzeb: The Life and Legacy of India's Most Controversial King; (Stanford University Press;2017), p.1
156 Kate Brittlebank, Tiger: The Life of Tipu Sultan; (Claritas Books; 2020), p.19
157 https://www.tutorhunt.com/resource/16208/
158 Shashi Tharoor, Inglorious Empire: What the British did to India; (Penguin Random House UK; 2017)
159 Sean Phillips, Why was British India Partitioned in 1947? Considering the role of Muhammad Ali Jinnah; https://www.history.ox.ac.uk/::og-node-637356::/files/download-resource-printable-pdf-3
160 Ibid.
161 Ayesha Jalal, Jinnah did not want partition; http://herald.dawn.com/news/1153717/jinnah-did-not-want-partition-ayesha-jalal
162 as cited in: https://herald.dawn.com/news/1153829
163 Khan Bahadur was the title of respect and honour given by the British gave to Muslim natives of British India
164 https://countrymeters.info/en/Indonesia
165 https://www.indexmundi.com/malaysia/demographics_profile.html
166 Dr Carool Kersten as cited in: https://www.trtworld.com/magazine/how-islam-came-to-dominate-indonesia-39182

167 Lakan Sumulong as cited in: https://peacebuilderscommunity.org/2016/01/understanding-the-moro-struggle-in-mindanao/
168 Renato Constantino, as cited in Ibid.
169 Omid Safi; https://www.baytalfann.com/post/islamic-art-more-than-aesthetics-a-path-to-the-divine-omid-safi
170 Rodney Gallop, The Origins of the Morris Dance, Journal of the English Folk Dance and Song Society, Dec., 1934, Vol. 1, No. 3 (Dec., 1934), English Folk Dance + Song Society; https://www.jstor.org/stable/4521040, pp. 122-129.

* 9 7 8 1 9 1 5 0 2 5 8 0 7 *
RE - #0010 - 280525 - C24 - 244/170/12 - PB - 9781915025807 - Gloss Lamination